Can God Move Here?

Can God Move Here?

A Quest for Revival in the Local Church

Toby Morgan

Book Editor: Wanda Griffith
Editorial Assistant: Tammy Hatfield
Copy Editors: Cresta Shawver
Esther Metaxas
Oreeda Burnette
Inside Layout: Mark Shuler

Library of Congress Catalog Card Number: 2001094126
ISBN:0-87148-218-5
Copyright © 2001 by Pathway Press
Cleveland, Tennessee 37311
All Rights Reserved
Printed in the United States of America

Dedication

To my precious family . . .

Diane,
my companion and the love of my life

my sons,
Stephen and *Andrew*.

Your presence in my journey has made
every step one of great joy.

Table of Contents

Foreword

Among a growing number of people, Toby Morgan is desperate to see a move of God in our generation. We are living in a time when the church is faced with the unique challenge of transitional congregations—people who are seeking demonstration instead of discipleship, entertainment over empowerment, and pastors who are swapping members of churches rather than winning new converts to Christ.

Pastor Morgan reveals the depth of his research by his awareness of what is happening around the world. He rejoices over the tremendous revival being experienced in South America. He is stirred by the overwhelming surge of God's Spirit in Africa, the almost unbelievable stories of evangelism in China, and the isolated outbreaks of God's Spirit at home.

The product of a church that has experienced a dynamic outpouring of God's Spirit, Pastor Morgan has heard challenging testimonies of the mighty acts of God in the past and seen edifices that testify of a bygone era.

With this background in mind, the author boldly asks the question: *Can God Move Here?* His prophetic pen challenges us to examine ourselves to see if we really desire God to move. He emphatically proclaims, "God can move and He will!"

As you read this book, you will be challenged by the author's forthrightness and conclusion—God is going to move, and it will be your decision as to whether you will be a part of His action.

I personally have been enriched by reading the burden of this concerned Christian leader as he speaks to the spiritual drought of our day. I know you will be touched also by his passion as you read this book. It is my prayer that the church in America will wake up and experience God's glory as never before.

—Dr. G. Dennis McGuire
First Assistant General Overseer

Introduction

Can God Move Here? was born of a passion to lead my church, Pathway Temple, and me into a new dimension of the Spirit of God. I have witnessed the Spirit of the Lord moving in an incredible fashion in other locales and pondered the same questions that nag many of us: "Why not here? Why not me? Why not now?"

This book seeks to answer some of these questions. It offers hope to those who earnestly pursue a deeper walk with God. Divided into three sections, Section One deals with the problems facing us, particularly in the American church, as God is pouring out His Spirit all over the earth. Using data from numerous sources, I have emphasized the need for revival in America. This salient point is made: God is pouring out His Spirit on the earth! Why aren't we experiencing the same outpouring as others? This section also deals with some sacrifices and commitments we must make in order to be a part of this great outpouring.

Section Two deals with places in which God will move. In spite of our reluctance to tread on dangerous ground, God has promised to pour out His Spirit in some rather hard places. These four chapters reference Scriptural examples that, from man's viewpoint, were impossible, and demonstrate how the Spirit of God is not limited to man's possibilities.

Section Three illuminates three great promises of God concerning this last-day outpouring. These thoughts challenge us to be committed to the task of preparation and participation in our final days.

If you are like me, you read the accounts of the great moves of God of our era. Who among us hasn't been startled by the statistics of the Brownsville revival? With a joyful heart, we rejoice over the thousands that have been saved. At the same time, we have a wistful longing for a move of God of that magnitude in our church.

I was privileged to listen to Steve Gray, pastor of the Smithton Church, where a tremendous outpouring of the Holy Ghost has been experienced. As I heard him speak, I wondered to myself, *Can God move in my church like he is talking about? Better yet, can God move in my personal life in a similar way?*

I will not presume to speak for anyone else when I say, "I need a mighty move of God in my life!" It is my hope that this book will motivate you to seek God for a greater move in your life and in your church. I am convinced God will propel you in unprecedented ways during these last days.

Today one deadly church sickness is our willingness to accept the status quo of religious mediocrity, while blaming it on the well-worn excuse, "The Bible tells us in the last days the love of many will wax cold and perilous times will come." That same Bible also says, "God will pour out His Spirit upon all flesh." We have only our lack of passion and desire to blame for our lukewarm existence as believers. God has so much more for us . . . providing we claim our inheritance as Spirit-filled believers.

Let's see what the hand of God will bring to pass as we join together and seek His face. Can God move here? You better believe it! Get ready for a great final-hour outpouring of the Holy Ghost.

section one

Our Problem

1

A Desperate Need for a Move of God

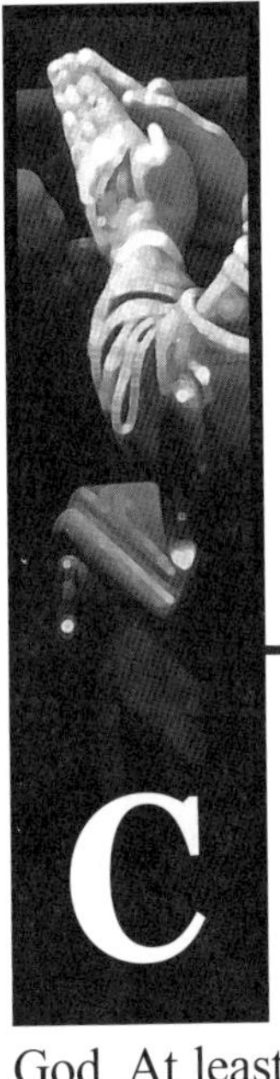

Can God move here?

What a question! Of course He can. God can do anything He wants, anytime He wants. After all, that's what makes Him God. At least that would seem to be the surface answer. God *can* move anywhere He wants. He can do things that are mind-boggling to us. He can accomplish things that are totally impossible to us. So, if God wants to move in my church and bring revival, He can.

Then why isn't God moving in a greater way in my life? Why isn't my church burning with revival fire? Why aren't thousands thronging to get through the doors of my church on Sunday? Why does it seem everyone else has the great spiritual breakthroughs? If these questions sound familiar to you, then perhaps we are on the same journey.

I am convinced God can, and will, move in my life, my church, my city. I think it is His will to move in ways we have never considered, or ways we once dreamed of and now have placed on the back burner. I think the Holy Spirit is preparing us for something great—a move of God like we have never seen! It is something I long for and believe can become a reality in our lives. Let's get ready for what God wants to do in these last days and prepare our hearts for what could very well be the last great move of God in the history of humankind.

In his powerful book, *soulTsunami,* Leonard Sweet provides graphic evidence of just how desperately the church needs a fresh move of the Holy Spirit. His chilling account of the pitiful state of the modern church makes this seminary professor sound like an Old Testament prophet. The following statistics help us realize the church's need for a fresh visitation of the Holy Ghost:

- Only India and China have more unbelievers than the United States, making the United States the third largest mission field in the world.[1]

- The Bible isn't closed . . . it's unknown. Biblical illiteracy is such that 12 percent of the American people think Joan of Arc was married to Noah. Eight out of 10 U.S. adults claim to be Christian, but they are hazy and lazy about their faith. Four out of 10 Christians are not able to name the four Gospels. Only half of those claiming to be born again read the Scriptures during the week.[2]

Add to this the steady drifting from God since the '60s when Christ was banned from our classrooms. The recipe for destruction is followed to the letter in our land.

It seems we have forgotten, or stopped believing, the words of the Spirit from long ago: "The wicked shall be turned into hell, and all the nations that forget God" (Psalm 9:17, *NKJV*). Without a move of God, this nation is running at breakneck speed into judgment. But before we organize demonstrations on the malls of Washington—demanding change and reform from men and women who cannot produce such—we need to focus on our own lives, our own churches. The sad truth is that the church needs a move of God more desperately than any government office or politician. The people of God must do more than just talk about revival: we must find a way to bring it into our lives. Revival can no longer merely be a catchy slogan for some conference—it must become our heartbeat. We—the church, the people of God—must rise to the occasion and rediscover the paths that lead to a fresh move of God in our lives. Then, and only then, will we have any hope of changing our world and seeing a great harvest of souls in these last days.

Sodom Needs an Abraham

Abraham is a perfect picture of today's church. He was a part of Sodom, but Sodom was not a part of him. He was the salty influence in that day which we must now be. Abraham didn't sit outside the fence and throw stones at Sodom; he modeled what we must do in our current situation:

1. By refusing to become like the people of Sodom, Abraham battled to save them.

2. He prayed for their salvation.

There is no better example of the church's task today. We must fight to save the world. We must rethink our methods and tactics and develop a "go-to-war" mentality. Rather than business as usual, we must allow the Holy Spirit to stir us to the point of battle.

Abraham was ready for the conflict. "When Abram heard that his relative had been taken captive, he called out the 318 trained men born in his household and went in pursuit as far as Dan" (Genesis 14:14).

He had 318 trained men. The Hebrew term in this passage means just that, *trained*. Abraham had looked out into the future and seen the possible need of men trained in battle. He realized difficult times could arise, so he prepared himself.

Are we training for war? Or are we soaking up the comfortable culture of American Christianity? If our eyes could only be opened to reality, we would see the true desperation of our times. Persecution of Christians is at an all-time high around the world. So pervasive is this persecution that one of every 200 Christians alive right now can expect to give their lives for Christ![3] That's a rather unsettling thought for those of us who perch on comfortable pews every Sunday morning, hoping the minister doesn't talk past noon because the restaurant cafeteria line might be too crowded.

With God's help, we need to be training ourselves and our children to stand in a time of war. If we are having difficulty standing for Christ today, what will happen when truly difficult times come? A question asked by the prophet Jeremiah applies today: "If you have raced with men on foot and they have worn you out, how can you compete with horses?" (Jeremiah 12:5).

Many will ascribe my sentiments to the rambling of some "far-right religious nut," but I am convinced, nonetheless, that the day is coming in the United States when immense pressure will be applied to the church which will force Christians to make a decisive stand for the Lord.

For some time, the United States has been moving away from God. Sometimes it is a slow, imperceptible crawl. Sometimes, it is a haphazard flight from the Lord.

While nations such as China and the former Soviet Union, and areas in Marxist-controlled Africa and oppressed areas of Latin America are experiencing great revival, with literally thousands of people being saved every day, a real move of God seems to evade us in America. On top of that, hostility toward a genuine experience with Christ seems to be mounting.

Those who think we can continue business as usual and "get along" with our sinful society need to rethink their stance. Like Abraham, we need to be training the church how to stand when the pressure is applied. Make no mistake, the pressure is coming! Consider these events, all of which occurred within a few days of each other:

- Vermont lawmakers approved a bill granting full acceptance to homosexual marriages.

- The 6th Circuit Court of Appeals ruled that the state of Ohio violated the U.S. Constitution with the motto, "With God All Things Are Possible." Incredibly, the ACLU lawsuit was filed by a Cleveland minister.

- Tufts University stripped a Christian Fellowship of all rights and financial funding because they refused a practicing and open lesbian a leadership position.[4]

As this nation becomes increasingly anti-Christian, we must emulate Abraham and prepare for what is coming. Simply going through the religious motions and being quasi-devoted will no longer ensure victory. We must come to the conclusion that a fresh anointing, accompanied by a Pentecostal move of God, is no longer a luxury for a few—it is a necessity for all.

The only way we can hope to save our generation is by going to war for souls—not with the sinners themselves but with Satan. Picketing, protesting and parading make us feel powerful, but these practices do not harm the kingdom of darkness. We must train to go to battle with spiritual darkness and wickedness in high places. One thing is sure—we better have the power of God in our lives if we plan to engage in this kind of warfare.

We must refuse the siren call of the world for acceptance. After Abraham won a decisive victory (something that only could have been done because of the hand of God, since he was outnumbered with only 318 men against four kings and armies), he would not partake of the wealth of the Sodomites.

> But Abram said to the king of Sodom, "I have raised my hand to the Lord, God Most High, Creator of heaven and earth, and have taken an oath that I will accept nothing belonging to you, not even a thread or the thong of a sandal, so that you will never be able to say, 'I made Abram rich'" (Genesis 14:22, 23).

He refused to allow the culture around him to corrupt his walk with God. It is distressing to see what happens in the church today. In an effort to become blessed, we have mistakenly associated wealth with blessing. We have adopted the tenet of our culture that says, "Rich is always best, and powerful is always right." Paul warned us about this:

> If anyone teaches false doctrines and does not agree to the sound instruction of our Lord Jesus Christ and to godly teaching, he is conceited and understands nothing. He has an unhealthy interest in controversies and quarrels about words that result in envy, strife, malicious talk, evil suspicions and constant friction between men of corrupt mind, who have been robbed of the truth and who think that godliness is a means to financial gain" (1 Timothy 6:3-5).

Good business is always in order. However, the church is not a business. We cannot afford to allow the kingdom of God to be measured according to the same standard as the corporate world. The bottom line is not profit versus loss for the church, and adopting the patterns set by Sodom simply so we can be rich is unacceptable. God and His plan for our lives must be the supreme standard against which we measure ourselves. If the world turns away from us, so be it. They hated our Master; how can we expect them to embrace us?

Just as we must not allow our lives to be caught up in materialism, neither must we allow our hunger for worship to diminish. In an attempt to become more palatable to a lost world and a dead religious system, many shy away from demonstrative worship. We seek to offer quiet, comfortable and culturally acceptable worship. Often, this is nothing but a tepid warm-up for our real demonstrations of love and joy—ball games, parties, social activities, and the list could go on and on.

If we are to have a move of God, we *will* be people who worship Jesus Christ with passion and sincerity, realizing that the words of Jesus are still true today: the way to run into God is through worship. "Yet a time is coming and has now come when the true worshipers will worship the Father in spirit and truth, for they are the kind of worshipers the Father seeks" (John 4:23).

Our Father is searching for people who will simply come to Him with all they possess and worship Him with reckless abandon. Amazingly, many of us are running in the opposite direction! Lou Engle tells of a conversation he had with a woman in an airport. He came around to asking her about her church affiliation and discovered she attended a Foursquare Gospel church. When Lou mentioned to her the great ministry of Aimee Semple McPherson, she promptly told him they were trying to get away from "that Pentecostal stuff." He then made a profound statement—one which we all need to contemplate:

> Spiritual amnesia happens when a denomination or the offspring of a particular move of the Spirit forgets the fresh revelation of Jesus Christ and the quickening encounter with the Holy Spirit that their forefathers and mothers embraced. The same doctrines are taught, but the power is not present. Whereas apostles first led the way, over time administrators became the leaders. Thus a whole generation arises that has never seen the power that birthed their inheritance.[5]

Never forget this: *A move of God is always associated with heartfelt worship.* Revivals, great moves of God, the sweeping wind of the Spirit, all come because the people of God decide to break out of predictable patterns of worship and give themselves over to the Spirit. God is looking for people who dare to worship Him. Can He find this kind of person in you?

Unless we are touched by the Holy Spirit and led by His divine plan, the tempting offerings of the world will be so alluring that we will not do as Abraham did and walk away—we will instead succumb to the pressure and accept the world's standards. When this happens, God will have no choice but to abandon us to our own decisions and allow us to reap the horrible consequences.

Finally, as Abraham prayed for Sodom, we must become consumed with intercession for our land. In Genesis 18, God revealed to him what was about to befall that wicked place. Had that been some of us today, we would probably have shouted, "Go, God! Burn 'em up! Fry 'em in the parking lot! They deserve it!"

That is probably one reason the world despises us; they know we have stored up venom for them and may strike at any moment. Not so with Abraham. Standing between the judgment of God and the wicked Sodomites, he interceded on their behalf.

The church must learn that our primary goal on earth is to stand alongside Jesus Christ and intercede for lost humanity. God doesn't need any more shouters, picketers, or red-faced, vein-bulging, hoarse-screaming protestors. He needs His children to hide away in prayer until His sovereign grace brings revival to the land. God is still looking for someone who will be that individual to stand in the gap.

It was a sad day when God searched for someone who would dare to stand and make a difference and He couldn't find anyone willing. The result, recorded in Ezekiel 22:30, 31, was tragic:

> "I looked for a man among them who would build up the wall and stand before me in the gap on behalf of the land so I would not have to destroy it, but I found none. So I will pour out my wrath on them and consume them with my fiery anger, bringing down on their own heads all they have done, declares the Sovereign Lord."

The church has become a great political army, but we have forgotten that coming together in prayer can shake nations. We have organized ourselves, marched in Jesus' name, protested amusement parks, screamed at abortionists; consequently, the world hates us with a passion. Perhaps the words of Joel apply to us today: "Let the priests, who minister before the Lord, weep between the temple porch and the altar. Let them say, 'Spare your people, O Lord'" (2:17).

Remember, God calls out to the church, not the world, to hide away in prayer until His Spirit empowers the church.

> "If my people, who are called by my name, will humble themselves and pray and seek my face and turn from their wicked ways, then will I hear from heaven and will forgive their sin and will heal their land" (2 Chronicles 7:14).

The only hope we have today is to see the hand of God move again in our church, our homes, our lives. We will never impress the world with our intellect, our organizational skills, our oratory or our wealth. We must simply have the power of God that fell at Pentecost come once more and carry us forward in a life-changing way.

2

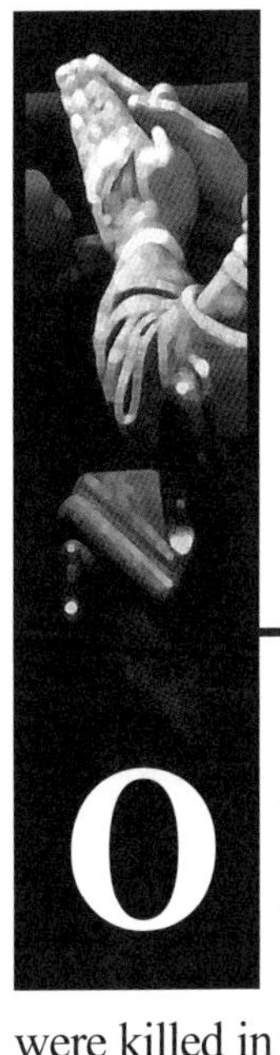

The Vision That Brings God's Glory

One early Sunday morning in May, just a few miles from where I live in Mobile, Alabama, there was a 20-vehicle pile-up on Interstate 10. Twenty-six people were injured and five were killed in this terrible tragedy.

It was discovered that an impairment of vision caused this catastrophe. Smoke from a three-day brush fire, coupled with a bank of heavy fog had reduced visibility to a minimum. In a matter of moments, buses, tractor trailers, cars and small trucks became tangled in a pile of burning junk. Because someone did not have proper vision, lives were forever altered in a terrible way.

A move of God requires that . . .

- Old patterns be broken

- Well-established Biblical methods that for ages have been set aside must be reinstated.

- A bold, new vision be embraced.

25

Embracing a bold, new vision has been the focus of previous generations who were seeking a glimpse of the glory of God. The ancient words uttered long ago by the wise man still reach us today: "Where there is no vision [revelation], the people perish [cast off restraint]; but he that keepeth the law, happy is he" (Proverbs 29:18, KJV).

Without a vision, without a fresh revelation of God, the people will go off the deep end—they will perish. They will lose touch with God unless they get alone with Him and discover the benefits of receiving a fresh challenge.

The church is filled with disobedient, rebellious people. Submission is a thing of the past. Church members rise up against pastors, and pastors attack their flock. Leadership tries to intervene and a fight ensues. Why? We have cast off restraint. We no longer have vision of the exalted Christ. We think we are serving a God who, if He has any power at all, is able only to keep us from hell . . . we hope.

In order to survive, we must see Jesus high and lifted up. This is our only hope. We must again envision a lost world, trekking at a maddening pace toward eternal damnation. We must see a Savior, bleeding for our sins. May God once again cause us to see a powerful, risen and ruling Jesus. If we fail to see Him, if we somehow miss this time of outpouring, we may lose this opportunity to be renewed and lead sinners to redemption.

I can identify with Jehoshaphat when he said, "O our God, will you not judge them? For we have no power to face this vast army that is attacking us. We do not know what to do, but our eyes are upon you" (2 Chronicles 20:12).

I do not have the answers to the pervading evil in our day. Neither do I know how to stem the tide of evil to bring about a great move of God in the church. I have heard what men say to do—I have even tried their methods, but have failed to get their results. Perhaps there is a lesson to be learned here. When we don't know what to do, we look to the One who does.

The situation looked grim for the people of God in Jehoshaphat's day. Alien armies were attacking, trying to wipe them from the face of the earth. Inferior in manpower, artillery and resources, the Israelites had no hope of winning the victory. But they realized what would ultimately lead them to victory.

This is the concept we must capitalize on today if we want to survive—we must take our eyes off the circumstances of the world and focus on a fresh vision of the glory of God.

What do you do when you don't know what to do? For the believer, the answer is simple. You simply go back and catch a new vision of God and what He wants. If we can only catch that vision once more, there is no limit to the wonderful things God can do through us.

A Vision of Inadequacy

One of our problems is that we actually think we are doing well. We believe we are making a powerful impact on our culture. "After all," we argue, "we have the greatest political influence the church has ever enjoyed in America. We who are called the 'religious right' can have a direct bearing on who is elected to public office and moves into the White House."

That may be a large part of our problem! We have taken the path of least resistance, addressing our problems in the same fashion as the world. The church has bought into the "might makes right" philosophy.

I fear we are merely caricatures of the early church. We are no more than a child's simple outline of what used to be a powerful influence for Christ. The words of Jesus apply to many more of us than we care to admit:

> "To the angel of the church in Sardis write: These are the words of him who holds the seven spirits of God and the seven stars. I know your deeds; you have a reputation of being alive, but you are dead. Wake up! Strengthen what remains and is about to die, for I have not found your deeds complete in the sight of my God. Remember, therefore, what you have received and heard; obey it, and repent. But if you do not wake up, I will come like a thief, and you will not know at what time I will come to you" (Revelation 3:1-3).

We think we are faring well, when in reality, we are simply holding down the fort, waiting for Jesus to come for us. How can we say we are doing well when the following truths stare us in the face?

- According to research done by the Barna Group, there are approximately 324,000 Protestant churches in the United States. With the average church attendance at approximately 100—incidentally, that is down from 102 in previous years—that means there are some 32,420,000 people in Protestant churches on Sunday.[1] That means that only just over one in 10 people in this country attend a Protestant church every Sunday.

- Andy Butcher reports the claims of revival in America are a myth. Believers' attitudes have changed little over the last 10 years. There have been no signs of increasing levels of interest in a relationship with God, in church involvement and in commitment to the Christian faith.[2]

- In the first few weeks between high school graduation and the day they enter a college's freshman survey, one in eight kids raised in church bolts from the fold.[3]

- The divorce rate in some areas of the church is higher than that of the surrounding world.

Let's face it. It is time for the church—that's us—to admit something . . . we haven't been doing a great job in the salt-and-light business. We just aren't getting it done!

Until we come to the point where we can admit our failure, we will never capture the fresh vision that is required to make a difference. We can certainly keep having church, tending to business, doing "Kingdom work," but we will never shake our nation for God without a new vision driving us forward.

Like Isaiah, we need to see our internal shortcomings. Notice what happened when Isaiah caught a fresh vision of God:

In the year that King Uzziah died, I saw the Lord seated on a throne, high and exalted, and the train of his robe filled the temple. Above him were seraphs, each with six wings: With two wings they covered their faces, with two they covered their feet, and with two they were flying. And they were calling to one another: "Holy, holy, holy is the Lord Almighty; the whole earth is full of his glory."

At the sound of their voices the doorposts and thresholds shook and the temple was filled with smoke. "Woe to me!" I cried. "I am ruined! For I am a man of unclean lips, and I live among a people of unclean lips, and my eyes have seen the King, the Lord Almighty" (Isaiah 6:1-5).

Isaiah was a man of God who heard from God and spoke God's message. But when he caught a fresh vision of the thrice-holy God, he began to understand his hidden shortcomings. He, along with the nation around him, was severely lacking in the things of God. Real truth, including the ability to make a clear and concise judgment of self, had been forsaken. Because of this clouded vision, underlying problems that needed addressing remained hidden. A vision of God's glory changed all that.

Suddenly, there was God—glorious, awesome, holy— so holy the angelic beings covered their eyes. When the prophet-scribe caught a vision of just how holy and upright God was, it occurred to him that he was the polemical opposite. He was lacking internal righteousness.

That's what seeing the Lord will do to you. It will cause you to fall on your face and confess your sins just as Isaiah did. The apostle Peter did the same.

When Simon Peter saw this, he fell at Jesus' knees and said, "Go away from me, Lord; I am a sinful man!" For he and all his companions were astonished at the catch of fish they had taken, and so were James and John, the sons of Zebedee, Simon's partners (Luke 5:8-10).

When Peter caught a vision of the glory and power of Christ, it stunned him so deeply he felt a need to repent. That's what seeing Jesus in power and glory will do.

Even Paul, the great apostle with a liberated heart, knew something of the utter failure of the flesh when it came to walking into the presence of the Almighty. "I know that nothing good lives in me, that is, in my sinful nature. For I have the desire to do what is good, but I cannot carry it out" (Romans 7:18).

The church must come to grips with the fact that many of us are not living the victorious, overcoming lives needed to demonstrate the glory of God. We need to once again see our Savior, high and lifted up in splendor and glory, full of power and might, conquering the forces of darkness and giving us power and the ability to overcome the enemy of our souls.

The first step is to see our need and allow Him to touch us. When Isaiah saw his need, he also witnessed the remedy. Hot coals from the burning altar of God were applied to his lips, and he was changed. When Isaiah allowed the Holy Spirit to purge him, he was transformed into a vessel that the Almighty could use. May God help us to see our inner need so that He can touch us as well.

We must also admit our *external inadequacies*. It is disturbing to realize that our world is coming apart and we don't know what to do about it. During the past 50 years, we tried to change our world with political influence and power, intellectual arguments and scholastic achievement, financial prowess and social programs—all of which have produced a weak church that has lost respect in today's society.

Like many in Scripture, we stand before a vast army with no knowledge of what to do. All our best efforts have failed. What do you do when you just don't know what to do? That was the position the people experienced in the day of the great leader Jehoshaphat.

When leaders of three nations came to attack him, Jehoshaphat stood helpless. He had no idea of what to do next. He needed a new vision, a new direction; he and the entire nation called on the Lord.

> Alarmed, Jehoshaphat resolved to inquire of the Lord, and he proclaimed a fast for all Judah. The people of Judah came together to seek help from the Lord; indeed, they came from every town in Judah to seek him (2 Chronicles 20:3, 4).

The next time a crisis hits close to home, we can look at this example. Pray, fast and solicit other people who will pray and fast with you. It sounds simple, but this strikes at the heart of our problem. We don't want to admit we can't fix the problem ourselves. I have found most believers are like me when I drive. The last thing I want to do is stop and ask directions—I don't want to admit I don't know where I am going.

Jehoshaphat didn't mind admitting he didn't know what to do. He prayed for guidance in front of the whole crowd. Picture Pastor Jehoshaphat, standing in front of a packed house on Sunday morning, praying this prayer:

> "O our God, will you not judge them? For we have no power to face this vast army that is attacking us. We do not know what to do, but our eyes are upon you" (2 Chronicles 20:12).

Most church councils would have called a secret meeting and tried to figure out how to get rid of him. Anyone who doesn't know what to do is out. But it was his admission of inadequacy that kept them from destruction! It was his cry of "Lord, I don't know what to do, but I am looking to You for help" that brought the ultimate victory in battle.

God gave Jehoshaphat a prophetic word. I like to call it "20-20 Spiritual Vision."

> Early in the morning they left for the Desert of Tekoa. As they set out, Jehoshaphat stood and said, "Listen to me, Judah and people of Jerusalem! Have faith in the Lord your God and you will be upheld; have faith in his prophets and you will be successful" (2 Chronicles 20:20).

Have faith in God, depend on His leading, listen to His Word, do what He says—He will deliver. That is what Jehoshaphat said that day, and that is precisely what the church needs to hear.

We need a fresh vision of faith. We have looked to Washington to deliver us, and have been utterly disappointed. We have labored under the delusion that technology would propel us into a greater harvest; and although in some cases it has been used wisely, the media fails to present a true message of the crucified Christ. We have even argued that if we had enough money, we would accomplish great things for God, forgetting that we are serving a God who owns the cattle on a thousand hills. We have been blessed in measures our forefathers could only dream of, yet we have not reached our nation for God.

We have tried it all, done it all, said it all, even spent it all, and still there is an army out there that hates us and seeks to relegate us to a corner. We don't know what to do, *but God does.*

We must trust His methods, allow Him to speak to us individually, and permit Him to direct our churches. Let Him give us the specific directions. The outbreaks of revival around our nation and the powerful ministries of anointed men and women have advanced the Kingdom. *But we need to place our faith in God and accept the plan He has just for us.*

A Fresh Vision

We serve a God of abundance. The apostle Paul wrote to the church at Ephesus: "Now to him who is able to do immeasurably more than all we ask or imagine, according to his power that is at work within us, to him be glory in the church and in Christ Jesus throughout all generations, for ever and ever! Amen" (Ephesians 3:20, 21).

Paul is saying, in essence, that God's power can exceed your dreams. We desperately need a fresh revelation of that truth.

When we go back to Isaiah's vision of the Lord, we can see how the prophet was moved when he took in the panoramic view of God's power. Just a glimpse of the awesome power of God caused Isaiah to fall on his face and tremble.

Years ago, William Barclay told us our God was too small. He was right. There is a desperate need for a new vision of the power of God. Teaching from so-called religious experts—men and women who deny everything in the Bible that cannot be explained—has raised questions about the power of God in the church. According to what many ministers are taught in seminaries across the United States, God is, at best, weak and incapable of powerful miracles; at worst, He is nonexistent. No wonder the church is unable to see the glory of God. No wonder our people are more interested in what happens on Superbowl Sunday night than what happens at church. Could this be why 40 percent of Americans claim to be born again, but slightly more than 10 percent of them attend church on Sunday?

Consider what the Bible says about God:

> The Lord is slow to anger and great in power; the Lord will not leave the guilty unpunished. His way is in the whirlwind and the storm, and clouds are the dust of his feet. He rebukes the sea and dries it up; he makes all the rivers run dry. Bashan and Carmel wither and the blossoms of Lebanon fade. The mountains quake before him and the hills melt away. The earth trembles at his presence, the world and all who live in it (Nahum1:3-5).

When Job caught a glimpse of His power, he was overwhelmed:

> His wisdom is profound, his power is vast. Who has resisted him and come out unscathed? He moves mountains without their knowing it and overturns them in his anger. He shakes the earth from its place and makes its pillars tremble. He speaks to the sun and it does not shine; he seals off the light of the stars. He alone stretches out the heavens and treads on the waves of the sea. He is the Maker of the Bear and Orion, the Pleiades and the constellations of the south. He performs wonders that cannot be fathomed, miracles that cannot be counted (Job 9:4-10).

Frank Damazio suggests that we bring stones out of our rivers just like Joshua and the people of God did when they crossed the Jordan. One of the modern stones we need, according to Damazio, is the stone of miracles and deliverance. "Participants in revivals around the world maintain the belief that physical, mental and emotional illnesses can be cured by the supernatural intervention of God through the prayer of faith. This stone must be grasped and held on to if we are to see healings and miracles move from the conferences and convention centers into our local churches."[4]

If we could only see the Lord as Mary did when the angel announced that she would have a child—Jesus. She knew it was biologically impossible, but she accepted the news with joy. Today we know that "nothing is impossible with God" (Luke 1:37).

This means:

- You can have a mighty touch of His anointing.

- Your church can come alive in the Spirit.

- Your loved ones can come to know Christ as Savior.

- Your sickness can be healed.

No matter how big your need is, God's abundant power is sufficient. It can happen!

What a change in attitude this can produce in us. We can be transformed from beggar to offspring of the King. No longer will we be limited by our small thinking and meager requests with a "hope-so" faith. We will dare to dream big dreams, make large requests and seek God with reckless abandon, knowing it is His pleasure to give good gifts to His children (see Matthew 7:11; Luke 11:13).

The World's Need

Many churches today are fat and self-indulgent. If we surveyed congregations with the probing question, "What is the primary purpose of the church?" many would say, "Take care of the membership." Others would answer, "To win the world for Christ." It is easy to see why there is so much tension between pulpit and pew. The truth is, most of us need a fresh vision like Simon Peter had on a hot rooftop.

Peter had been praying and fasting for a season when the Lord opened heaven before him:

About noon the following day as they were on their journey and approaching the city, Peter went up on the roof to pray. He became hungry and wanted something to eat, and while the meal was being prepared, he fell into a trance. He saw heaven opened and something like a large sheet being let down to earth by its four corners. It contained all kinds of four-footed animals, as well as reptiles of the earth and birds of the air. Then a voice told him, "Get up, Peter. Kill and eat." "Surely not, Lord!" Peter replied. "I have never eaten anything impure or unclean." The voice spoke to him a second time, "Do not call anything impure that God has made clean." This happened three times, and immediately the sheet was taken back to heaven. While Peter was wondering about the meaning of the vision, the men sent by Cornelius found out where Simon's house was and stopped at the gate. They called out, asking if Simon who was known as Peter was staying there. While Peter was still thinking about the vision, the Spirit said to him, "Simon, three men are looking for you. So get up and go downstairs. Do not hesitate to go with them, for I have sent them" (Acts 10:9-20).

Simon saw things to eat which had never touched his lips—things strictly forbidden in his kosher diet. He knew to keep away from them because they were not Judaically acceptable.

Then God upset matters. The men Peter encountered soon afterward were very much like the food items he had seen in the vision. They were outside his field of acceptance. He had never partaken of any of them. Now, God was telling him to get ready to adjust not only his taste buds, but also his vision of the world harvest. God was beginning to save Gentiles.

Notice what happened after Peter started preaching to them:

> While Peter was still speaking these words, the Holy Spirit came on all who heard the message. The circumcised believers who had come with Peter were astonished that the gift of the Holy Spirit had been poured out even on the Gentiles. For they heard them speaking in tongues and praising God. Then Peter said, "Can anyone keep these people from being baptized with water? They have received the Holy Spirit just as we have." So he ordered that they be baptized in the name of Jesus Christ. Then they asked Peter to stay with them for a few days (vv. 44-48).

Immediately the church was not just a Jewish group, but it had people who were vastly different. God was saying to them, "The harvest field is the world."

It's time we understand that while the message must forever be the same, our methods can, and must, change. Perhaps it's time to ask ourselves some really tough questions:

- How much of our church budget goes to taking care of those of us who are well fed and secure in Christ, and how much goes to winning the lost?

- How open are we toward those who don't look like us?

- What would we do if the order of things in a service changed to make us more aware of newcomers?

- How are we reaching out to the lost in our surrounding area?

- How much do we give to world missions in any given year?

- What am I doing to evangelize those around me?

Even the apostle Peter had to be shaken from the doldrums of self-centered, everybody-has-to-be-like-me religion. He had to receive a new vision of the lost world around him. Perhaps it's time we crawl up on that roof with God and let Him touch our hearts as well.

One thing is certain: If we fail to capture the vision of God for our day, our generation will scarcely know we were here. God is too great and our task too large for us to allow this to happen.

3

Four Stops on the Road

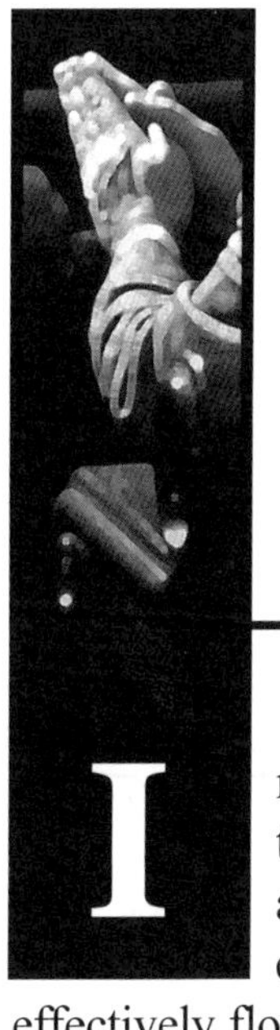

In this desperate day, we need much more than the standardized church service. Only a double portion of God's anointing can elevate us to the place where God can effectively flow through us. What we need is typified in the Old Testament story of Elisha's anointing.

> When they had crossed, Elijah said to Elisha, "Tell me, what can I do for you before I am taken from you?" "Let me inherit a double portion of your spirit," Elisha replied. "You have asked a difficult thing," Elijah said, "yet if you see me when I am taken from you, it will be yours—otherwise not" (2 Kings 2:9, 10).

The world, desperately seeking the "spiritual," is ripe for the deception of the Enemy. A hint of something different, something supernatural, will cause the world to flock around a person like pigeons eating bird seed in a city park. All the while, the Evil One is making inroads on every hand.

We were shocked to read about a teenager in Huntsville, Alabama, who brutally murdered his mother, father and siblings with an ax. His friends said he had changed from a great guy to someone capable of committing this crime about the time he became involved in occult practices. The source of his problems is easily recognizable. Satan's influence is unmistakable across the globe today.

Everyone is painfully aware of the horrifying violence of the school shootings at Columbine. As experts scratch their heads, asking how these young men could commit such a dastardly crime, the answer comes from the killers themselves. Their disdain for Christ and their seething hatred for believers unmasked the truth: They were driven by demonic powers, the influence of which we cannot begin to grasp.

In light of these contemporary expressions of evil, the church must be more than a group of nice people who come together on Sundays and then make a mad dash to their favorite restaurant. It is time for us to be light—real light. It is time for us to be salt—salt with savor. When will we move from our comfortable pens and become sheep among wolves?

Some time ago the phrase "sheep among wolves" caught my attention. It is set in the context of Jesus' giving a commission to the Twelve: "I am sending you out like sheep among wolves. Therefore be as shrewd as snakes and as innocent as doves" (Matthew 10:16).

This same commission applies to Christians today. Jesus calls us from our comfortable places of worship to do His ministry—to be sheep among wolves. When sheep venture out among wolves, they are devoured. Does Jesus want us to be torn apart by Satan and his forces? The answer is a resounding "No!"

The complete account is recorded a few verses earlier in Matthew 10: "He called his twelve disciples to him and gave them authority to drive out evil spirits and to heal every disease and sickness" (v. 1).

He did not send them out as meek lambs, destined to become wolf lunch. Rather, He gave them power over the kingdom of darkness, sending them out as turbo-charged rams, full of the power of God. They were equipped with power to take on the strongest demonic strongholds and bring them crashing to the ground.

The good news is that we have been promised the same power. We are called to become lambs, not peacocks. The peacock attitude repulses people before they ever get close enough to hear the message. Neither are we to haphazardly blunder like a bull in a china shop. That makes the world despise us. We aren't even supposed to go out like an eagle to target some sinner and drag him into the Kingdom. People are insulted that we consider them something to be harvested for God. No, we are to be like lambs—meek, lowly, self-effacing, approachable—offering something of substance to those who don't know Christ.

When the wolves come howling, we need not worry, because beneath the cuddly exterior of wool lies a breastplate of righteousness, a helmet of salvation, a belt of truth, shoes of peace that give stability, a shield of protection and a sword to slice the howling predator.

We are not defenseless.

"But you will receive power when the Holy Spirit comes on you; and you will be my witnesses in Jerusalem, and in all Judea and Samaria, and to the ends of the earth" (Acts 1:8).

Jesus has promised us power that enables us to attack the wolves and defend our territory.

1. Jesus wants us to take the salve of healing into the territory of the one who makes us sick.

2. Jesus wants us to take the message of deliverance into the prison of the devil.

3. Jesus wants us to take the glorious news of grace into the house of despair created by Satan.

4. Jesus calls His church to shake the gates of hell, setting the captives free.

5. Jesus calls us to march into the burning house of drug addiction, alcoholism, sorrow and despair, screaming at the top of our lungs, "Come this way to rescue! Follow me to freedom!"

To do this, we *must* have a double portion of God's anointing. Without this anointing, our words will fall flat and the Enemy will devour us before we ever get started.

Even though he was close to the master, Elisha desired more power in his life. I think that is the place so many of us find ourselves in today. We know we need more of God, but we fail to allow Him to move in our lives.

If you fit this description, please read on. There is a power, an anointing, awaiting you on your journey. However, some of the stopovers are rough and difficult to overcome. The journey can get rocky, but those who stay on course will find a divine empowerment awaiting.

Elisha's answer was simple—just be present when Elijah left the earth. That's all. Just be there. Sounds like an easy appointment, but Elisha was in for a long day. Several stops in his journey to a double-portion anointing lay ahead.

Stop One: Gilgal

"When the Lord was about to take Elijah up to heaven in a whirlwind, Elijah and Elisha were on their way from Gilgal" (2 Kings 2:1). The day started with the twosome traveling from Gilgal. What is the significance of this place?

At that time the Lord said to Joshua, "Make flint knives and circumcise the Israelites again." So Joshua made flint knives and circumcised the Israelites at Gibeath Haaraloth. Now this is why he did so: All those who came out of Egypt—all the men of military age—died in the desert on the way after leaving Egypt. All the people that came out had been circumcised, but all the people born in the desert during the journey from Egypt had not. The Israelites had moved about in the desert forty years until all the men who were of military age when they left Egypt had died, since they had not obeyed the Lord. For the Lord had sworn to them that they would not see the land that he had solemnly promised their fathers to give us, a land flowing with milk and honey. So he raised up their sons in their place, and these were the ones Joshua circumcised. They were still uncircumcised because they had not been circumcised on the way. And after the whole nation had been circumcised, they remained where they were in camp until they were healed. Then the Lord said to Joshua, "Today I have rolled away the reproach of Egypt from you." So the place has been called Gilgal to this day (Joshua 5:2-9).

Gilgal was the place where the people who had wandered in the wilderness for 40 years were circumcised. Today Gilgal represents the place where we celebrate our liberation from Egypt, the place where we come to Christ. It is the time in our lives when we come under His lordship and embrace the sanctified life.

Some of us need to stop our frantic activity to camp for a season at Gilgal and settle an important question: Is Jesus the Lord of my life, or do I worship the job? Regrettably, many of us linger at Gilgal while glory awaits in the Promised Land. Rather than submitting to the One who called us, we still want control.

I am suspicious of the "partial surrender" salvation we hear about so often. This business of making him "Savior" but not "Lord" may play well in religious circles, but it certainly is not Biblical. Throughout Scripture, He is both Savior and Lord. It cannot be "either/or"—it must be both.

Until we come to Gilgal and fully commit to Jesus Christ, we haven't even started down the road to a double-portion anointing.

Stop Two: Bethel

"Elijah said to Elisha, 'Stay here; the Lord has sent me to Bethel.' But Elisha said, 'As surely as the Lord lives and as you live, I will not leave you.' So they went down to Bethel" (2 Kings 2:2).

On their way out of Gilgal, the twosome stopped over for a quick breakfast at McDonalds. Elijah has Elisha order him some pancakes and sausage (maybe eggs instead of sausage). While Elisha is standing in line to get the food, Elijah gets that far-off look in his eye. He tells the younger man, "You stay here and eat. God has called me over to Bethel."

"No way," he said. "Where you go, I go." By insisting on accompanying Elijah, Elisha demonstrated the tenacity required to move into the anointing he sought.

I find it interesting that there is a mountain between Bethel and Gilgal. We will soon see them retrace their steps back over the mountain to Jericho. Is the Lord showing us something here? Is there something we have missed? Crisscrossing that mountain took stamina, energy and commitment. Could it be that one of the major reasons we fail to move into a powerful walk with God is that we tire so easily and do not possess the drive required to propel us forward when the going gets tough? Elisha never questioned why. He never complained about the harshness of the journey nor the seeming replication of steps back and forth across the mountainside. He simply moved when his master moved. Oh that we could develop such a tenacity!

Why Bethel? What could that mean to us? Let's look at what happened there:

> He [Jacob] had a dream in which he saw a stairway resting on the earth, with its top reaching to heaven, and the angels of God were ascending and descending on it. There above it stood the Lord, and he said: "I am the Lord, the God of your father Abraham and the God of Isaac. I will give you and your descendants the land on which you are lying. Your descendants will be like the dust of the earth, and you will spread out to the west and to the east, to the north and to the south. All peoples on

earth will be blessed through you and your offspring. I am with you and will watch over you wherever you go, and I will bring you back to this land. I will not leave you until I have done what I have promised you." When Jacob awoke from his sleep, he thought, "Surely the Lord is in this place, and I was not aware of it." He was afraid and said, "How awesome is this place! This is none other than the house of God; this is the gate of heaven." Early the next morning Jacob took the stone he had placed under his head and set it up as a pillar and poured oil on top of it. He called that place Bethel, though the city used to be called Luz (Genesis 28:12-19).

Jacob and all the people with him came to Luz (that is, Bethel) in the land of Canaan. There he built an altar, and he called the place El Bethel, because it was there that God revealed himself to him when he was fleeing from his brother (35:6, 7).

Bethel is that place in your life where God becomes real to you. It is that place where the Lord begins to reveal Himself in a breathtaking way, the place where you begin to realize that following the Lord can sometimes lead to some rather unexplainable events in your life.

It is wonderful to know there is a place beyond Gilgal, although some people never leave. They are engrossed in the pain and suffering of coming out of Egypt. It makes them feel good, I suppose, to dwell on the negatives. They like the feeling of punishment in their spiritual journey. Not me. I thank God for Gilgal, but I don't want to go back there. I want to move on to Bethel and sense the mystery and glory of God.

It's fun at Bethel! Most Pentecostal and Charismatic believers want to camp here because we like it so much. As a matter of fact, we are addicted to the place. We love the manifestations—tongues, prophecy, visions and dreams. We enjoy seeing ladders ascend to heaven and sensing so much of the presence of God that our hair stands on end. We are like the speaker in Job, when the presence of the Almighty came close: "A spirit glided past my face, and the hair on my body stood on end" (4:15).

Aren't you glad God reveals Himself to us in power and glory? Aren't you glad God doesn't hide in a corner and shout at us, "See you when you get to heaven!"?

I love to sense the fire of God's presence when He moves. The visitation of the Holy Ghost is an amazing feeling, but we can't stay at Bethel just to have a good time. We need to move on with the Lord.

Just about the time Elijah and Elisha settle in at the pizza buffet for lunch (remember, they left breakfast on the counter this morning), Elijah starts to get that funny look in his eye again. He tells the young prophet, "Stay here and enjoy lunch; I sense God calling me somewhere."

Stop Three: Jericho

"Then Elijah said to him, 'Stay here, Elisha; the Lord has sent me to Jericho.' And he replied, 'As surely as the Lord lives and as you live, I will not leave you.' So they went to Jericho" (2 Kings 2:4).

Back across the mountain they went to a city most of us are somewhat familiar with, thanks to Sunday school lessons.

Now Jericho was tightly shut up because of the Israelites. No one went out and no one came in. Then the Lord said to Joshua, "See, I have delivered Jericho into your hands, along with its king and its fighting men" (Joshua 6:1, 2).

Jericho is the place God will lead us to set the captive free—the place where we start the spiritual battle. Jericho is the place where the power will begin to flow through us, enabling us to bring captives out of the kingdom of darkness and into the kingdom of light.

There is something interesting in the first verse of Joshua 6. Note that the city was said to be "shut up." That didn't mean it was quiet, although it probably was. What it really meant was that no one was going in or coming out. There was no movement at all. The enemy, in this case, the Israelites, held them in bondage and fear.

Regrettably, some of us have a tendency to think, *Fine! That's what they deserve! Bunch of sinners! Hope God lets 'em have it with both barrels!*

We would never verbalize that opinion because of the vengeful and grim tones it produces, but that's the way a great number of us feel about the lost world.

If you believe I am mistaken, or quick in judgment, please consider the following questions:

1. Why aren't we doing whatever we have to do to have a move of God that would set the captives free?

2. Why are we so self-absorbed and passively ignorant of the vast harvest around us that is not being touched for the kingdom of God?

A number of years ago, when working on a church staff, I led a large group of senior adults on a Christmas party. After dinner at a restaurant on the outskirts of Birmingham, Alabama, the group decided to ride back through the city and view the Christmas lights. It was a gorgeous night. The only problem was that in the area of some of the brightest Christmas lights, there were some other lights burning—red ones! That's right, I took a group of senior adults down a beautifully decorated street inhabited by a group of prostitutes. Etched forever in my mind is the cold and cynical comment made by one of our "dear saints." "They ought to burn," she said, almost hissing. I responded something to the effect of, "Well, Merry Christmas to you, too."

I have thought about that comment many times since that cold December night. That lady told the truth—they should burn. But that is only half the truth. Not only should they burn, so should we! If we would be honest, we would recognize that all have sinned and come short of the glory of God. We have the right to judge no one.

What should motivate us is the fact that Jesus died for everyone, including the prostitutes on that street. Included in that vast group for whom Jesus suffered are homeless people in our cities, those with a different skin color, even those who smell bad and don't fit in with our society. The fact that Jesus loves each person we meet enough to lay down His life for them should stir us until we see our need for a fresh visitation from the Holy Spirit.

Here is something that should keep comfortable Christians in nice, neatly packaged little churches awake at night. There was someone there in Jericho, one family that caught the eye of God. This family was headed by, of all things, a prostitute!

Can you believe that? Rahab caught the eye of God and He saved her and her family. It wasn't the mayor, the governor, or even one of the "bluebloods" of Jericho whose family came over on the *Mayflower.* No, God saved a prostitute from off the streets!

Isn't it time we caught on to the fact that God loves the poor, the down-and-outers—all the nobodies without a chance in this world? Think of it—right in your city are drunkards, drug addicts, prostitutes, men addicted to pornography and women sitting on bar stools who have caught the eye of God. He wants to set them free, but He is looking for a church through which He can pour out a mighty wave of His glory and power, leading to salvation.

My desire is for my church to become a double-portion church where the Rahabs of our day can find deliverance. I want to slip a red cord into the crumbling buildings of our society and shout, "Here's the way to deliverance!"

I know we are not going to win them all, but I am convinced there is a Rahab out there in my city, who sits huddled with her kids tonight, wondering if life offers any hope. I want to throw a scarlet rope to her and let her know there is a way out. I want her to know Jesus Christ will set her and her family free!

Out there somewhere is a young man, thinking life is over. All he can see is that crime pays enough to live, as long as he doesn't get caught. I want to throw a scarlet thread to him and let him know Jesus will change his life!

All around us are people bound by drugs, enslaved by alcohol, living day-to-day in hellish bondage and seeking escape. They want out. We, the church of the living God, have been placed here to show them the way.

Why would God want to give us more of His glory just to spread around the local church? We are saved, delivered, out of Jericho already. We don't need any more glory in the confines of the church if all we are going to do is run around and prophesy to each other so we can feel good on Sunday. We don't need a double portion of God's power so we can come together and have "good church." We have proven over and over that having a nice service without God's deliverance is possible. It happens every Sunday when we meet and go through the motions without ever touching the throne of God. We are going to need the extra anointing of His Spirit if . . .

- We visit the hospital and pray for someone dying with AIDS.

- We go to get out and tell someone else about Jesus.

- We come up against the power of the Enemy.

- We enter into intercession.

- We attempt to set the captive free.

Stop Four: The Jordan

"Then Elijah said to him, 'Stay here; the Lord has sent me to the Jordan.' And he replied, 'As surely as the Lord lives and as you live, I will not leave you.' So the two of them walked on" (2 Kings 2:6).

It's late afternoon by now. Elisha left breakfast and lunch on the table in order to follow Elijah; and now, just before the fried chicken and mashed potatoes are delivered, Elijah gets that crazy look one more time. He looks over at Elisha and says, "Son, you stay here and eat. God has called me to go to the Jordan."

Again, we see the dogged determination required to move into a deeper walk with God. Elisha says, "I've told you once, I'll tell you again. Where you go, I go." So, off they trekked toward the Jordan River.

We all know what Jordan represents, don't we? Jordan represents death—the "crossing over." We must catch a glimpse here of something vital and indispensable if we are going to have a double-portion move of God. *Elisha was to face "death" before he could be the vessel God could use.* He faced it, and so will we. There are some things you are going to have to die to if you want to move on with God. We, as the church and individually, must make the decision to die. A church must make the decision to die.

Denominations fare no differently. It all boils down to this: Are we willing to die in order to live in the Spirit?

1. *We must be willing to die to public opinion.* If we really want to experience the glory of God, we must come to the point we don't care what the world thinks about us. Sadly, that's rarely the case. Here's what can happen. A church is blessed of the Lord and begins to grow. With growth, we gain some people of influence and wealth, perhaps the mayor or even a congressman. Sometimes we have millionaires in our pews. If we are not careful, we begin to worry more about what *they* think than what *God* thinks. We become concerned with what the secular press has to say about us. We even worry about what those on television say about us. We have begun the journey that causes us to lose touch with God.

We need to understand something up front: *the world isn't going to like us!* This can clearly be seen in the way

Elisha was mocked in his day. Even after serving them, Elisha suffered ridicule from unbelievers.

> The men of the city said to Elisha, "Look, our lord, this town is well situated, as you can see, but the water is bad and the land is unproductive." "Bring me a new bowl," he said, "and put salt in it." So they brought it to him. Then he went out to the spring and threw the salt into it, saying, "This is what the Lord says: `I have healed this water. Never again will it cause death or make the land unproductive.'" And the water has remained wholesome to this day, according to the word Elisha had spoken (2 Kings 2:19-22).

Through the power of God, Elisha brought about this wonderful miracle in their midst, and touched each life. He gave them drinking water, and they still mocked him. It wasn't long until some of the younger ones were making fun of the man of God.

> From there Elisha went up to Bethel. As he was walking along the road, some youths came out of the town and jeered at him. "Go on up, you baldhead!" they said. "Go on up, you baldhead!" He turned around, looked at them and called down a curse on them in the name of the Lord. Then two bears came out of the woods and mauled forty-two of the youths. And he went on to Mount Carmel and from there returned to Samaria (vv. 23-25).

They were poking fun at him, challenging him to go up in a whirlwind like Elijah had done. Did you know God has a way of taking care of things like that? Two bears came down from the wooded hillside and ripped 42 of them to pieces!

That may sound terrible to you. Some of us want to know, "How could a loving God do something like that?" I guarantee you they were only parroting what they had heard dear old Mom and Dad say at home! Learn a lesson and be careful about what you have to say concerning the work of God.

I know some people who have criticized everything about the church their entire lives:

- "That good-for-nothing preacher"

- "That pitiful church staff"

- "That boring teacher"

- "That off-key singer"

- "That terrible song selection"

- "That lamentable choir"

Nothing is good enough! Then they wonder why their kids, who have heard the criticisms all their lives, won't come to that sorry church and hear that lousy preacher preach and that lamentable choir sing.

There's a valuable lesson to be learned here: Be careful what you have to say about a move of God. God still has some bears He can use to silence critics of His work, should He choose to do so.

What happens when people in the Kingdom allow negative opinions of others to dominate their thinking? We slink off in a corner somewhere and whimper about how the world excludes us. We start whining about how unacceptable we are and actually start buying into the mantra of society that demands openness and flexibility in every area of life except those the church holds dear. Then, before we realize it, in an effort to gain acceptance by a godless society, the church changes to accommodate the world that holds nothing but contempt for the Christ we love.

I don't mean to sound pompous with an air of superiority, but the church needs to develop the attitude that says, "Who cares about public opinion? It will change tomorrow. We are serving an unchanging God!"

Let the world laugh at us. Let the so-called intelligentsia mock us. Let the religious fast-frozen of the world talk about us. Ignore their hollow words and pursue God with a white-hot passion!

2. *We must prepare to die to religious usefulness if we are seeking a double-portion anointing.* If you start to move in the things of God, the religious world will throw you out, telling you how you have gone off the deep end. They will eviscerate you with scathing denunciations, all based on "love," of course. What that means is while they are kicking you out, they will finish their scourging with "Jesus loves you." If you are going to experience a deep move of God, get ready for it.

Here's how religion treats a move of the Holy Ghost:

> The chief priests and the teachers of the law heard this and began looking for a way to kill him, for they feared him, because the whole crowd was amazed at his teaching (Mark 11:18).

Jesus came in the power of the Spirit, stirred things up, turned over some of their theological applecarts, and they couldn't handle it. They wanted to kill Him, ending the move of God they considered threatening. That same thing is going to happen in your life when God touches you. People who used to like being around you won't hang around anymore. They will talk about how weird you have gotten. Some people in church world, perhaps in your local place of worship, will start to criticize the "crazy" ways you are acting.

Why will people in church act this way? Religious people don't want a move of God and they don't want you to have one either. Since it's easier to kill off a double-portion anointing than to go through all the trouble of obtaining one they really don't want in the first place, the next logical move is to get out the guns and start firing at anything that moves.

If you really want to have a move of God, you have to go to Jordan and die to selfish desires! A move of God, a double-portion anointing, will take over your life.

Suppose God really shows up at church next Sunday. I mean, God *really* shows up. People get saved. People who have been coming to church for years get saved. Someone gets healed. Some are baptized in the Holy Ghost. Someone is delivered from drugs. Someone else is set free from the bondage of pornography. Great things happen all over the house.

Guess what's going to happen next?

- Your time is no longer your own.

- Your parking spot will be taken next week.

- Your seat will be occupied when you stroll in next time.

- Our nice, neat, predictable little service won't be the same.

- Our cozy, comfortable, little church won't ever be the same.

- Suddenly, crowds of people will show up and inconvenience you.

They will come because a move of God brings healing. There is a hurting world out there that needs healing so badly they will try anything. When God shows up in the church and they find out about it, they will crawl over each other to get in.

The story of Bud Williams, an Episcopal priest in Lakeland, Florida, in his book *Fire in the Wax Museum*, illustrates my point. Hungry for a move of God, Bud sought the Lord and invited Him to come into his church. One day God accepted Bud's invitation and showed up. Things started happening that had never happened in his church. Folks started staggering like drunk men under the influence of the Holy Spirit. Laughter erupted. So did weeping. Services lasted for hours as people were caught up in the move of God. It was a reflection of Pentecost, a move of God.

When God moves, some things must go to Jordan and die. One of those things is the selfish desires of people. These are Bud's own words about his trip to the Jordan:

The biggest change came not from what we took away but from what we added. People wanted more praise and worship, altar calls and the laying on of hands every Sunday. In many ways, it was a pastor's dream; in another, his worst nightmare—it added a lot more time to the service. The main service was already pushing two hours, but with this expanded liturgy, it frequently lasted more than three. I knew this was hard on mothers with young children, elderly folk, and those who could not sit for a long time. One man complained regularly about missing the buffet at the retirement home. It was a problem only God could solve, and He did so.

A revelation struck me like a thunderbolt: The members of the congregation were grownups! If they could not sit, they were free to move around. If the service ran too long for them, they were free to leave or to come to the early-bird special (this was their name for an early morning service). If someone missed his lunch, he could either go to McDonalds afterwards or bring a sack lunch with him. The point is, we stopped trying to please and manipulate people and sought instead to reverence God and yield to whatever He desired to do in the church.[1]

The last sentence from Bud Williams is the key for any church desiring a real move of God. We must die to our own selfish desires for the church and yield ourselves to the Spirit of the Lord like dead men yield to those who bury them. We must let God do what God wants to do. I am convinced He wants to dramatically move in our lives. Let's follow Him and see what He will do.

<h1 style="text-align:center">4</h1>

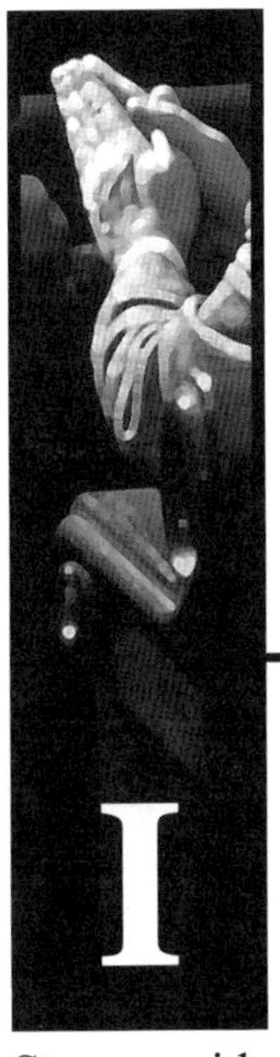

Taking the Limits off God

It was a Monday afternoon after a powerful service on Sunday night. As a matter of fact, I cannot recall a church service in which so much of the power of God was manifested. Strong evidences of the Spirit of God were all over the place. People broke forth in shouting. Others danced and laughed. Over in one corner of the building, people knelt and wept while on the other side of the room, people were standing with hands raised toward heaven.

I was flat on my face in an altar area for at least one hour, pressed under such a heavy weight of the glory of God I did not have the strength to stand. Struggling to my hands and knees to stand up from the tear-soaked carpet, I noticed there were about half a dozen men gathered around me. Some were still seeking God while others were lying on the floor in the atmosphere of the Holy Ghost. It was the strongest surge of God's awesome power I have ever sensed. No one worked it up. No one sang it down. No one manipulated the congregation.

There were about 300 of us there that night when God simply invaded the church and took over.

I must make an honest confession to you. That night set me on fire for something greater of God. I have never been the same since that night. I can't honestly tell you I have dwelled in a thick presence of God since then, but as Tommy Tenney so aptly put it, "I have been chasing God ever since!"

As great as that Sunday night was, Monday afternoon in prayer rocked my world even more. After making several hospital visits, I stopped by the sanctuary on my way to the office and lay before the Lord, offering Him thanks for the powerful visitation on Sunday night. Out of nowhere, my loving Father began to rebuke me. That's right, the Holy Spirit began to chastise me on the day after I had been caught up in the Spirit. Here's what the Lord spoke to my heart that afternoon: "Morgan, what I did last night was nothing! You are limiting Me and I will be limited by no man! Get out of My way and I will move!"

I don't know how long I lay there and wept that day. I only know it was one of those "breakthrough" times with God. It is burned indelibly into my heart and I will never forget that afternoon. I sensed God touching my life as never before. In the midst of that prayer time, the Lord burned several areas of my life with hot coals from the altar. I think I felt something like Isaiah did when the hot coals were applied to his lips.

Then one of the seraphs flew to me with a live coal in his hand, which he had taken with tongs from the altar. With it he touched my mouth and said, "See, this has touched your lips; your guilt is taken away and your sin atoned for" (Isaiah 6:6, 7).

I was singed, burned. Some ways that I was limiting God were brought to the surface. When He touched those places in my life, I flinched. It hurt! However, when I yielded to His scorching hand, it changed the way I saw God and what He can do. I suspect many of us have built those boxes in our lives. We have constructed, over time, our own little boxes where we expect God to dwell. Maybe you are like I was. I thought I was fairly open to a move of the Spirit and accessible to what God wanted to do, but I had caged the Almighty. That day I learned something . . . *God is too big for my box!*

I was guilty of placing restraints on the Lord by my own estimation of His ability. I would sing "God can do anything" with one breath, observe God move, and then develop the attitude, *That's as good as it can get.* I was limiting God's power and goodness.

Looking back, I can see how silly I really was. In my classical Pentecostal upbringing, I would witness a move of the Holy Spirit, look over to my brother in the Lord who disagreed with me and thought I had gone off the deep end and say to him, "You are limiting God!" He would respond, "No! It's you who has gone off the deep end. I have all I will ever need in salvation by the blood and the Word of God." I would say, "No, there is more! Take the limits off God!" He would counter, "No! My pastor says all that stuff died out when the Bible was written. My Sunday school teacher says you are all a bunch of crazy people, or worse, demon-possessed." Naturally, I assumed he was limiting the way God could move; so I would leave the discussion with a smug sense of "spiritual superioritis."

Now, it gets really interesting. Once I walked away from that argument, self-assured of my victory, I would run into a brother who talked about a move of God I hadn't experienced—mighty things of God that had eluded me. So, what did I do? I would start picking at his theology, trying to find some little crack in his doctrinal armor, frantic to discover some error in his preaching, some "flakiness" in his way of doing things so I could feel smug and comfortable in my "contented Pentecostalism."

I hate to admit this, but I was doing the very thing I was accusing my non-Pentecostal brother of doing. In essence, I was saying to God, to Almighty God, "I am the benchmark against which all You do must be measured." I actually had the nerve to think that.

No, I never said it, or actually realized I believed it, until God broke into my life and said, "Stop boxing me in!"

If you are reading these words and thinking to yourself, *Well, he just doesn't care about good doctrine or theology,* think again. Everything I believe and hold dear comes from God's Word. My problem was not, and is not today, the trashing of God's Word. Rather, it is a selective acceptance of God's Word. If we believe the witness of Scripture given by Scripture itself—and by that I mean that all Scripture is God-breathed and useful—then we must come to grips with the fact that the God we encounter in the Bible is quite capable of doing far more than any of us could ever dream possible. Our accomplishments pale in comparison to this awesome God we serve. We must, as pastors and leaders of today's church, be honest and admit that we are not making a great impact on today's culture. Admitting that, we must stop making excuses for our lack of success, throw away our rationalizations of our failures, and start on a course that will lead us into more of the glory of God.

We serve a fantastic God who cannot be contained by our puny, man-made systems. If you think you have cornered the market on God, think again. He goes beyond anything we have ever heard or seen. Let these simple truths sink in.

Consider this powerful story of God's fantastic provision:

The hand of the Lord came upon Elisha and he said, "This is what the Lord says: Make this valley full of ditches. For this is what the Lord says: You will see neither wind nor rain, yet this valley will be filled with water, and you, your cattle and your other animals will drink. This is an easy thing in the eyes of the Lord; he will also hand Moab over to you. You will overthrow every fortified city and every major town. You will cut down every good tree, stop up all the springs, and ruin every good field with stones." The next morning, about the time for offering the sacrifice, there it was—water flowing from the direction of Edom! And the land was filled with water (2 Kings 3:15-20).

Verse 18 drives home the point: "This is an easy thing" in the sight of God. It was nothing for Him.

Our God can even make the sun go backward!

Isaiah answered, "This is the Lord's sign to you that the Lord will do what he has promised: Shall the shadow go forward ten steps, or shall it go back ten steps?"

"It is a simple matter for the shadow to go forward ten steps," said Hezekiah. "Rather, have it go back ten steps."

Then the prophet Isaiah called upon the Lord, and the Lord made the shadow go back the ten steps it had gone down on the stairway of Ahaz (20:9-11).

God is so powerful, were He to withdraw from us, we would shrivel up and die on the spot.

If it were his intention and he withdrew his spirit and breath, all mankind would perish together and man would return to the dust (Job 34:14, 15).

Our God is far above anything that concerns us:

He sits enthroned above the circle of the earth, and its people are like grasshoppers. He stretches out the heavens like a canopy, and spreads them out like a tent to live in (Isaiah 40:22).

He is such an awesome God, no one can stand before Him: "But the Lord is the true God; he is the living God, the eternal King. When he is angry, the earth trembles; the nations cannot endure his wrath" (Jeremiah 10:10).

I think the psalmist describes Him best: Our God is in heaven; he does whatever pleases him (Psalm 115:3).

We puny mortals actually think we can stop Him or alter His plan. But God can do anything He wants, at any time He decides. Therefore, when we look on a move of God and say, "That's as good as it will ever get," we are limiting Him, boxing Him in. With God, there is always more!

Now to him who is able to do immeasurably more than all we ask or imagine, according to his power that is at work within us, to him be glory in the church and in Christ Jesus throughout all generations, for ever and ever! Amen (Ephesians 3:20, 21).

Paul is telling us we can't think it, dream it, conjure it in our imagination, have it dawn on us, get together and plan it out . . . *but that our God can do it and more!* If we will take the limits off God, He will do more through us than we ever dreamed possible.

I had to learn to take the restraints off the Spirit of the Lord. God spoke to me very forcefully about how I needed to change. See if any of these changes come home to you.

Limiting God by the Priority of Time

I have always been time-conscious, worrying about how long a service was running. When it got too close to 12 on Sunday morning, I would start fidgeting, worrying about who was getting upset over the length of a service. I didn't realize it, but I was limiting God by the hands on my watch.

On a typical Sunday morning, I was accustomed to giving the Lord approximately 75-90 minutes to move. If He couldn't get it done between 10:45 and 12:15, He wasn't going to get it done. I had already moved on. On Sunday nights, I was a little more liberal with God. I gave Him as much as two hours to accomplish the impossible. How magnanimous I must have appeared in heaven.

God spoke to me that Monday afternoon. With profundity and weightiness, He told me, "Morgan, I will not be rushed!" I learned something that day. God doesn't need a long time to do something powerful, but He can take it, if He wants to.

Have you ever thought of what Paul said concerning the coming of Jesus in Bethlehem?

"But when the time had fully come, God sent his Son, born of a woman, born under law" (Galatians 4:4).

Jesus came in God's own good time. Not one year earlier. Precisely when God declared the time to be right, Jesus came forth. Men who had looked for the Messiah all their lives were dying without seeing the Promised One, but in God's own good time, Jesus came.

This struck me that day: Who am I to say to God, "You have until 12:15 to move, or I am out of here"? I really wonder how many times we have walked out just about the time God was about to move. I wonder how many services I have cut short because I could sense the people were wandering mentally and I was about to lose them. How many times might five more minutes of worship have brought about such a stupendous move of God that a great revival would have broken out?

I am not advocating long, drawn-out services for the sake of spending time. No, what I am trying to get across is the notion that God's schedule and ours can be different. What would have happened if the early church had decided to leave the Upper Room on the ninth day and not returned for day 10? They would have missed God! Thankfully, they stayed "until," and Luke recorded how they shook the world.

When the day of Pentecost came, they were all together in one place. Suddenly a sound like the blowing of a violent wind came from heaven and filled the whole house where they were sitting. They saw what seemed to be tongues of fire that separated and came to rest on each of them. All of them were filled with the Holy Spirit and began to speak in other tongues as the Spirit enabled them (Acts 2:1-4).

Note when this great move of God happened, Pentecost came. Luke described it as the swamping of a boat with water.

The Spirit moved when the time was right. They had to cast off restraints of time and tarry before the Lord in order to experience the mighty move of the Spirit. Do we honestly think we can demand God to show up on our timetable? A thousand times no! Let's stop being in such a hurry and stop worrying about those who feel they need to leave. Instead, let's learn to tarry in His presence and give the Lord ample time to move in our hearts.

Limiting God by My Preconceptions

As I alluded to earlier, I was as bad as some of my colleagues who thought I had gone off the theological deep end. I thought, without saying it, *If it isn't my way, it's the wrong way.* Even now, some of you are amazed at such a confession. Don't look so smug. Some of you are just as bad as I ever was! The truth is, we all come to the table with our own neatly packaged, tightly wrapped set of preconceived ideas about how God works. Heaven forbid for someone to tell us the Lord moved in their life in a different way than He did in ours.

Do any of these ideas sound familiar to you?

- When I was saved, I cried a puddle of tears on the altar. Does that mean no one else is really saved unless they cry?

- When I received the baptism in the Holy Ghost, I spoke in tongues for half an hour. Does that mean someone who only speaks a few phrases with "stammering lips" didn't receive the same Holy Ghost?

- When I was growing up, the Holy Spirit would move and we would dance around the pot-bellied stove. Am I to believe that the Holy Spirit only moves where we dance and have old-fashioned means of heating a building?

God is not relegated to the way He "used" to do things. Remember the words of Jesus:

"But about the resurrection of the dead—have you not read what God said to you, 'I am the God of Abraham, the God of Isaac, and the God of Jacob'? He is not the God of the dead but of the living" (Matthew 22:31, 32).

Our God is not stuck in the way it used to be. He is a living, today, right-now God. That means He is far beyond my meager preconceptions.

My upbringing was in a great church that had a solid youth program. The choir I sang in was tremendous. We made tours every summer and sang in churches all over the United States, and even outside the country. The music program was leading edge for the time in our denomination. I was nourished under great pastors—men who loved God and cared for the flock. I was privileged to have wonderful Sunday school teachers who instructed me in the Word of God. Church services were filled with tremendous singing, anointed preaching and powerful worship. In reflection, I was given about as good a chance of knowing Christ and becoming a disciple as one could have had. However, I grew up with the opinion that if church services were to be blessed of the Lord, they had to mimic the ones I had known as a teen. In other words, sing until the glory of God fell on us. No preaching meant a great service.

As time passed, God, in His wisdom and providence, called me to do something I thought was going to kill me—God had me pack up and move. As much as I hate to admit it, they did fine without me. God began the teaching in my life He continues to this day. He was letting me know that my preconceived ideas were not necessarily the standard by which everything else was to be judged.

Like most young men in the ministry, I started out as an evangelist. Traveling to mostly small congregations, I soon discovered there weren't many places that sang the glory down like they did back home. It struck hard at my "it has to be this way" mentality. I will never forget one night in Ferriday, Louisiana. It really was a "God moment" in my life. I was conducting a revival for the 10 or so saints who were faithful enough to endure my preaching. One night the singing was not all that great. I remember vividly sitting in the chair, dwelling on how sad the service was, when it dawned on me: *God can move in this place with or without a great music program!*

I can't explain that feeling to you; you have to experience it for yourself. Suffice it to say that the Holy Spirit quickened me. We did have a move of God that night. Not only that, I made a startling discovery: I love great music; I want a great music program; *but God can move in a powerful way without one!*

Perhaps you are like I was. I had to abandon all my preconceived ideas about what it takes to have a move of God.

- He can move when there is great music like He did when Elisha called for the musicians, or He can move without the sound of music like He did when Elijah prayed down fire on Mount Carmel.

- He can make His presence known when a great preacher is preaching like He did with Peter in the house of Cornelius, or He can make His presence known when a layman like Philip goes down to Samaria.

- He can show up powerfully when a bunch of saints are praising Him like He did on the Day of Pentecost, or He can show up in the middle of a bunch of sinners like He did with Saul on the road to Damascus.

- He can appear and bring the dead to life as He did with Dorcas, or He can bring the living to death as He did Ananias and Sapphira.

- He can show up and make the earth quake to set a preacher free like He did Paul and Silas, or He can come by and open the eyes of a dying saint so they can see Jesus like He did with Stephen.

- He can show up through laying on of hands, spitting and making clay, or pouring out oil. He can come like a gentle dove or a roaring hurricane, like a refining fire or a gentle voice, like a mighty river or a healing stream, like a hot wind from the desert or a rock in a weary land.

Who are we to say how He is to do His business? I really don't care if He shows up like a river, a stream, a flood, a fire, a tornado or a dove . . . just as long as He shows up!

Limited by Power

Finally, I limited God's power. I have always been one of those who accepted at face value the statement "God can do anything," but I had become so analytical in my faith, so demanding for an explanation of everything that I was on the verge of becoming a skeptic. I knew God could; I just wasn't sure God would.

Don't misunderstand me. I am not in favor of checking your brain at the door when you enter the church. I believe our faith should be analyzed (to a point), but analyzed with this presupposition: There are things in the kingdom of God that simply cannot be quantified or qualified in the same manner as some scientific theory. There is simply no way to explain many of the things found in Scripture, or in life for that matter, apart from faith. If you sit around and pick everything apart from a humanistic point of view, you might well miss a great move of God in your life.

It's time for us to get back to the God of the Word who possesses more power and might than we will ever experience. Who do we think we are to limit His awesome ability by telling Him "You can only move in this way or on that person"? That's like telling a thunderstorm where it can pour out rain and where it cannot. The thunderstorm is going to rain anywhere it finds conditions right, and our God is going to move in power and glory where He finds conditions to His suiting.

During the Gulf War, a newscast displayed a small protest group gathered at the Golden Gate Bridge outside San Francisco. By that time, about 99 percent of America was in favor of President Bush's actions in the Gulf.

However, this small group decided to protest. What struck me was not the fact of their protest, but the rationale they used. Their argument was that the President of the United States did not have the right or power to send troops to battle. They were sincere, but sincerely wrong.

It's a solemn thing to consider, but the man we elect as president every four years has at his disposal the most horrifying and destructive weapons of war imaginable. He can, without consent from anyone else, send Marines or Navy SEALS to wage war on any continent on earth. Overnight, with a simple order, he can send Air Force or Navy fighter planes into action against any target on the planet.

That small group just off the Golden Gate Bridge was claiming the president did not have the right or power to mobilize the military, but they were wrong. The president does have that right.

Do you know what was happening while they were lying around on the pavement? Bombs were falling all over Iraq. Cruise missiles were zipping through the streets of Baghdad. Troops were amassing on the border. Tanks were being put into place. In spite of protesters telling the president what he couldn't do, he was doing it all the time.

That's just like some of us in the Kingdom. We are busy telling the King what He can't do, and He's busy doing it! While we are telling Him how He can't cause people to fall before His glory, He's moving all around the world and people are falling before Him. While we are shouting at God about how He can't cause us to laugh, people are laughing in the Spirit and obtaining victory. While we have been running around declaring to God how He can't fill others, (especially Catholics) with the Holy Spirit, God has been pouring out His Spirit in such a lavish manner that the Catholic church is now the largest Pentecostal denomination on earth!

As much as I hate to burst the bubble for some of us, God has the power to do things in people's lives without questioning us and getting our approval—and He's been busy doing just that!

This quote from Benny Hinn illustrates my point:

As we continued down the corridors of the hospital, we passed a visitor's lounge filled with people. Some were sitting there smoking, some were talking, and some were watching the "Phil Donahue Show." My friend, the priest . . . looked at me and nodded toward the lounge area, indicating he thought we shouldn't overlook these people. Obviously, they had no idea who we were, although it was apparent something was happening. We entered the lounge and began to anoint each of the visitors. One by one, they fell under the power. In fact, as we began to pray for one gentleman who was smoking, he fell under the power with a lit cigarette still in his mouth.[1]

Before the Lord dealt with me, I would have had some problems with that statement. Some of you also have problems with that statement. You might love Benny Hinn, but it bothers you. Let's see if you can identify with my feelings:

- A Catholic priest who wasn't Spirit-filled was praying for people and they were falling under the power of God.

- It wasn't a church or a chapel.

- There was no worship music, only a television blaring—of all things, Phil Donahue.

- They were smoking.

- One man, apparently touched by the Lord, was smoking when it took place.

If I am not careful, I will tell the Lord:

- You can't move on people like that.

- You can't move in a place like that.

- You can't move in a predicament like that.

God shouts back at me, "WHO DO YOU THINK YOU ARE TO TELL ME WHAT I CAN AND CANNOT DO! TAKE THE LIMITS OFF, MORGAN!"

In my struggle to become all God wants me to be, I am coming to the place where I believe God will do anything. In days to come, He will move in ways that stagger our imagination. He will show up when we least expect Him. Are you open for a greater touch, or are you satisfied with what you have? I confess. I know there has to be more. With this God I serve, there is no limit. I long for a deeper touch. I am ready to disassemble my little box and see what this awesome God can do. Anybody want to get their wrecking equipment and join me?

5

How Broken Are We Willing to Be?

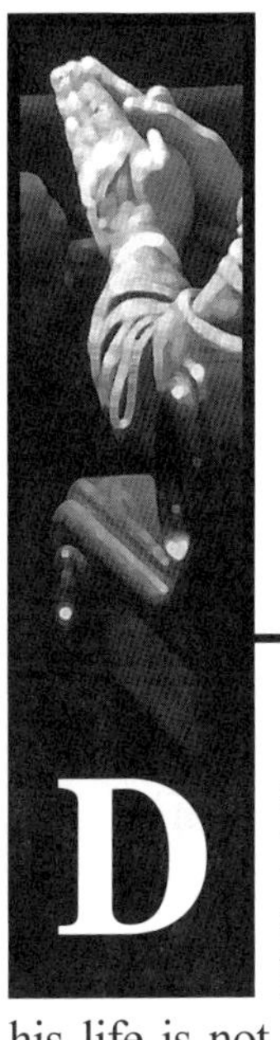

David makes some alarming statements in Psalm 69. He was broken, insulted and offended. His life had been assailed by turbulent circumstances. What was going on in his life is not all that uncommon, but the reason for this upheaval is downright disheartening. David was broken because He experienced a move of God in his life.

> For zeal for your house consumes me, and the insults of those who insult you fall on me. When I weep and fast, I must endure scorn; when I put on sackcloth, people make sport of me. Those who sit at the gate mock me, and I am the song of the drunkards (vv. 69:9-12).

All he was trying to do was follow hard after God. All he wanted was to know the Lord better. He was hungry for a move of God. You would think the Lord would thunder from heaven with the zeal of David for His house, and pour out such power and anointing that the servant king would be vindicated. Were I God, David would have heard nothing but angelic music and glory from on high. Instead, he heard the insults of the people. The word *insult* means carping, upbraiding, defaming, blaspheming, railing and defying. Here was a man seeking God and he was finding trouble from those around him. On top of that, he became the butt of their jokes. He was the one they sang about down at the local tavern. He had become a man they did not understand.

The worst part is that the main leaders of the mob against him were the people within the house of God! They were satisfied with the status quo and wanted nothing to do with changes. They liked life as it was, and this "newfound passion for God" was upsetting their nice little church.

No wonder Jesus quoted this psalm one day when He made an unannounced visit to the house of God. You can find the details in John 2. In a divine rage, He flipped tables over and sent money rolling everywhere. Turning from those, He smashed open bird cages and released doves. Finally, in what seemed to those standing around to be the work of a mad man, He ran them out with a whip, like angry bees being forced from their hive. John then added this commentary: "His disciples remembered that it is written: 'Zeal for your house will consume me'" (John 2:17).

My question has been, and remains, *"Can God move here?"* Before we give our standard "yes" answer, we need to ask ourselves another question, "How deeply are we prepared to be broken?" Here's why: If you aren't ready to be broken, you are not ready for God to move in your life.

God only uses broken things to do His work. He only moves through broken vessels. Vance Havner, that great preacher of old, said, "God uses broken things. Broken soil to produce a crop, broken clouds to give rain, broken grain to give bread, broken bread to give strength. It is the broken alabaster box that gives forth perfume. It is Peter, weeping bitterly, who returns to greater power than ever."[1]

Are we willing to allow the Holy Spirit to break us, to cut us deeply, to bend us to the will of God, making us pliable enough to flow through us? Our fate, and the fate of our children—indeed the fate of many around us—hinges on our response to that question.

Misconceptions About a Move of God

Many of us labor under false pretense about the Lord showing up in our lives. We think it is all about blessing, wealth, honor, status, or some other fleshly thing. All we can think about is the Lord moving in a great way so everyone will know how really "in touch" with God we are. And that, my friend, may be one of the main reasons we don't see God move in our churches.

The idea of God moving mightily in our lives sounds pretty good, until we look beneath the surface. Most all of us will eagerly say, "Yes! I want a move of God!" That is, until that move of God starts to reveal the sin we have concealed. Suddenly, we reverse the course and say, "Wait a minute! Who does He think He is, making those demands on me? After all, that's just the way I am."

Here's some sobering news . . . He is God! And He has every right to deal with us any way He wants to.

We have many misconceptions concerning a move of God:

- When God moves in my life, I am going to get rich.

- When God moves, I am going to get that Cadillac.

- When God moves, I am going to have such a good time.

- I can't wait for God to really move in my life, because when He does, I am going to shout for joy!

How wrong we are! A genuine move of God is going to result in some of us getting so broken in His presence that others in the church start making fun of us. They are going to joke and laugh behind our backs.

Let's take a moment to trace the course of some people's lives when God moved. It is a trail of brokenness.

Isaiah

Isaiah was a member of an influential, upper-class family. He was educated, had great gifts and was personally acquainted with royalty. The most literary of the prophets, he married a woman who also was gifted in prophetic gifts. He was a part of a great aristocracy in the land.

Did Isaiah have a move of God in his life? You better believe he did! No one foresaw the coming of Jesus like Isaiah. But chapter 20 of the book bearing his name reveals something which had to break the man:

In the year that the supreme commander, sent by Sargon king of Assyria, came to Ashdod and attacked and captured it—at that time the Lord spoke through Isaiah son of Amoz. He said to him, "Take off the sackcloth from your body and the sandals from your feet." And he did so, going around stripped and barefoot. Then the Lord said, "Just as my servant Isaiah has gone stripped and barefoot for three years, as a sign and portent against Egypt and Cush, so the king of Assyria will lead away stripped and barefoot the Egyptian captives and Cushite exiles, young and old, with buttocks bared—to Egypt's shame (vv. 1-4).

God had the princely prophet walk around barefooted and naked for three years. He had to bear the insults of people and listen to the whisper of the slanderers for three years. He had to endure the joking rebukes of the community for three years.

Why would God do such a thing? It's simple. Before God flows through you into the life of someone else, He first breaks you and molds you in the image He wants.

The modern church, especially the American church, would have written Isaiah off as a nut or given a sanctimonious appraisal of the "judgment of God" on his life. "After all," we reason, "if God was in what was going on in his life, not only would he not be naked, he would be wearing the finest new suit money could buy." And we would miss what God was doing by a country mile! God help us to wake up and realize that all that glitters is not gold and we need a move of God more than anything else on earth.

Mary

This young teenage girl was minding her own business, preparing for her upcoming wedding. All at once, out of nowhere, an angel pops up with news from heaven. If I could produce an angel and get him to tell you things, people would line up for miles in every direction and throw money at my feet like I was a god . . . *unless they really listened to what the angel had to say.* Listen to what this one told Mary:

> In the sixth month, God sent the angel Gabriel to Nazareth, a town in Galilee, to a virgin pledged to be married to a man named Joseph, a descendant of David. The virgin's name was Mary. The angel went to her and said, "Greetings, you who are highly favored! The Lord is with you" (Luke 1:26-28).

Talk about a move of God! When Gabriel, the one who stands in the presence of Jehovah, shows up to personally deliver a message, that's a move of God! What he told her was astounding. "Mary, you are highly favored in heaven. The Lord is with you."

I'll be honest. As a man of God, there is nothing I own I would not gladly lay on the altar to have that same experience. I suspect most of us are in agreement with that.

What comes next is even more astounding:

> "You will be with child and give birth to a son, and you are to give him the name Jesus. He will be great and will be called the Son of the Most High. The Lord God will give him the throne of his father David, and he will reign over the house of Jacob forever; his kingdom will never end" (vv. 31-33).

Shocked out of her mind, Mary states the obvious:

> "How will this be," Mary asked the angel, "since I am a virgin?" The angel answered, "The Holy Spirit will come upon you, and the power of the Most High will overshadow you. So the holy one to be born will be called the

Son of God. Even Elizabeth your relative is going to have a child in her old age, and she who was said to be barren is in her sixth month. For nothing is impossible with God."

"I am the Lord's servant," Mary answered. "May it be to me as you have said." Then the angel left her (vv. 34-38).

What a move of God! The Lord is doing the impossible in her life. It's great. Wonderful. Powerful. Wouldn't we all love to have an angel show up today and tell us the news, hot off the presses in heaven, "God really likes you! He is going to do the impossible in your life!"?

But wait—that's not where the story ends. She does conceive and bear a son. When they take the baby Jesus to the Temple to dedicate Him to God, they meet up with an old prophet named Simeon. Listen to what he had to say.

Then Simeon blessed them and said to Mary, his mother: "This child is destined to cause the falling and rising of many in Israel, and to be a sign that will be spoken against, so that the thoughts of many hearts will be revealed. And a sword will pierce your own soul too" (Luke 2:34, 35).

That last line disturbs me. "A sword will pierce your own soul too." I want to ask her, "Mary, is it still 'May it be to me as you have said'?"

- It's one thing to see your son turn water into red wine at a wedding, but another to see his blood spill forth like wine from a cross.

- It's one thing to see your son being clamored around like insects to a light, it's another when they all leave and only a handful remain.

- It's one thing to see your son raise a dead man from the grave, another to see your son die and be buried.

- It's one thing to hear your son talk about grace and forgiveness, another to stand around while lying men lynch him on trumped-up charges.

Her heart was crushed by that mighty move of God. But, before the Messiah could come, someone had to be willing to be broken. Someone had to be willing to pay the price required.

The Apostle Paul

Here's a guy who, as soon as he gets saved, is confronted with some breaking of his own. After all, how many of us were struck blind when we first came to Jesus? The Lord sends one of His servants down to pray for Saul, later called Paul, with this message:

But the Lord said to Ananias, "Go! This man is my chosen instrument to carry my name before the Gentiles and their kings and before the people of Israel. I will show him how much he must suffer for my name" (Acts 9:15, 16).

Paul had to be willing to be broken in order to have God flow through his life. It becomes obvious that he has some rather trying times ahead. His life was not going to be about private jets and exclusive book deals. No, the greatest apostle the world has ever seen was broken and spilled out until he finally met the Master in heaven.

Moldable Clay

Here's the salient question: Are we willing to be broken, to be molded into the image of God? Let's face it, some of us have grown rather hard in areas of our lives. I remind you, it is the moldable clay that becomes the vessel the potter desires. Only when God can break us, change us, bend us, will He move in our lives.

What about our pride? Are we willing for that to be broken? Our pride is the major reason we do not see a great move of God in America today. We are actually so full of ourselves we think we don't need God. We can do just fine without all that "spiritual stuff."

One of the characteristics of the Laodicean church was that they were "rich, and increased with goods, and [had] need of nothing" (Revelation 3:17, KJV). How can any of us dare to have one iota of pride left when we remember how our Savior died? We have this picture of Jesus, a few drops of blood coming out of the corner of His mouth, a nice garment wrapped around his midsection. He is way off, up on a hill with a few people milling around.

Recent studies revealed that is not at all what happened. Actually, the Lord was on a beam about 18 inches off the ground, right by the busiest thoroughfare in the city. People were everywhere. He was stripped of His clothing and beaten almost to death. Naked. Humiliated. Broken. *But that's what it took for God to move in the earth and save you and me!* Understanding that immense pain and breaking in His life, how can we allow our pride to hinder a move of God?

How about position within the body? Are we willing for that to be broken? You know what I mean—our seat of authority, our influence, our prestige. Some of us are so intent on keeping "my place" we may actually hinder God's anointing flow in the church.

One day, Jesus was graced by a visit from the mother of James and John. She wanted Jesus to grant them a great "position." It would be nice to be seated right there beside Jesus, or so she thought. Jesus put a different spin on things. "'You don't know what you are asking,' Jesus said to them. 'Can you drink the cup I am going to drink?' 'We can,' they answered" (Matthew 20:22).

They had no idea what kind of brokenness that would bring. To their credit, they drank the cup. But the move of God cost them all they had. Are we willing to be broken for the Lord's glory?

A Great Challenge

There's a strange passage of Scripture found in Matthew 21. Jesus has just described Himself as the stone the builders would reject but which would later become the chief cornerstone of the building (v. 42). Then Jesus made a dramatic statement: "He who falls on this stone will be broken to pieces, but he on whom it falls will be crushed" (v. 44).

There is an interesting difference in the two actions presented here. In the latter activity, what the *New International Version* calls "crushed," there is the idea of smashing up and winnowing. In other words, there is a separation. It is like taking a clay pot, smashing it up, grinding it into powder and then throwing the dust in the air. In other words, once this has happened, there is no possibility of future use. You might as well forget it. The pot is marred beyond repair.

On the other hand, the word *broken* has the idea of breaking up and mixing together. It carries the idea of smashing something up together. Those who love to cook are familiar with this idea. It is the same concept as taking grain and smashing it up, creating a flour. After that, you mix in some other ingredients and make a cake or bread.

I think this verse puts us squarely at a place of decision. Either we fall at the feet of Jesus, the chief Cornerstone, and get broken, or the stone will fall on us and crush us to pieces. Either we allow the Lord to mold us, break us, do with us as He pleases and then flow through our lives, or He will move somewhere else and we will be crushed into useless powder. If we fall before Him, He will raise us up and make us the vessel of His choosing. If we stiffen, He will crush us and render us useless.

As individuals, and the church, we must come to the place we either fall upon Jesus and allow Him to make the broken pieces in His image, or continue to resist and wait upon the stone to fall upon us, bringing the judgment of God.

The results of our decision are too far-reaching to make the wrong choice. Time is swiftly flying by and the Lord God has given us a proposal. We can come before Him and accept His touch, or we can insist on our own way and suffer the consequences. The response we make to God's offer has eternal repercussions. We simply cannot afford to continue with business as usual.

Jon Allen tells the story of a summer spent with grandparents. Rummaging through the attic one day, they happened upon some old *Life* magazines. One stark black and white photo was of a visibly broken Nebraska farm family. It seems their small son had wandered out of the house into the surrounding wheat fields. Since he was so small, the tall shafts of wheat obscured him from view. Frantic, the father and mother searched all day. Finally, at dusk, they called for their neighbors. Through the long, cold night the men searched with lights and lanterns. Photos showed them in a human chain, walking with hands clasped, in ever widening circles. Finally, around noon the next day, they found the little boy. He had died sometime during the previous night.

The last picture showed the father, tears streaming down his dirt-covered face, carrying the body of his precious son from the fields. He was quoted as saying, "If only we had joined hands sooner he could have been saved."[2]

Our generation is faced with the same desperate predicament. Looming on the horizon is the cold darkness of the coming judgment of God. Now is the time to join with the Lord, to partner with the Lord in work, as Paul alluded to in 1 Corinthians 3:9. It is time to become committed to, even frantic for, a great move of God. Our hour has arrived to come in complete submission and surrender to the Lord and experience a fresh outpouring of His holy fire. We, along with the next generation, cannot afford anything less than a great move of God.

The question really isn't "Can God move here?" The real question each of us faces today is much more personal. It's time for every one of us to evaluate our lives with this standard: "Am I willing to be so broken before the Lord He can put me back together and flow through me?" Only you can answer that question.

Places God Will Move

6

God Will Move in Deserted Places

The desert and the parched land will be glad; the wilderness will rejoice and blossom. Like the crocus, it will burst into bloom; it will rejoice greatly and shout for joy. The glory of Lebanon will be given to it, the splendor of Carmel and Sharon; they will see the glory of the Lord, the splendor of our God. Strengthen the feeble hands, steady the knees that give way; say to those with fearful hearts, "Be strong, do not fear; your God will come, he will come with vengeance; with divine retribution he will come to save you." Then will the eyes of the blind be opened and the ears of the deaf unstopped. Then will the lame leap like a deer, and the mute tongue shout for joy. Water will gush forth in the wilderness and streams in the desert (Isaiah 35:1-6).

In stark contrast to the future of the unrepentant and rebellious people stands the future of those who welcome God into their hearts. There is a blossoming desert. As a replacement for the arid, uninhabitable climate, the believer has something wonderful. In a place where nothing welcoming has been for a long time, those who experience a move of God can have a lush paradise of the glory of God.

This is a picture of many of us in the Kingdom. So many of us are in a deserted place, a wilderness where it seems no one cares or understands. From all appearances, even God doesn't know where we are.

Thirsty, lonely, even scared, we wander around in a daze, searching for some glimmer of hope.

Isaiah described us, and promised us something wonderful from the Lord:

> The poor and needy search for water, but there is none; their tongues are parched with thirst. But I the Lord will answer them; I, the God of Israel, will not forsake them. I will make rivers flow on barren heights, and springs within the valleys. I will turn the desert into pools of water, and the parched ground into springs. I will put in the desert the cedar and the acacia, the myrtle and the olive. I will set pines in the wasteland, the fir and the cypress together, so that people may see and know, may consider and understand, that the hand of the Lord has done this, that the Holy One of Israel has created it (41:17-20).

God is telling us He knows how to move in deserted places. He knows how to show up in the arid times of our lives, in those times when we feel deserted and alone. God can even show up in those days when it seems He is a million miles away. In the dry, deserted places of life, God knows how to make water flow. He knows how to bring the shouts of joy back into the dead places.

I love what the Lord says He is going to bring: the glory of Lebanon and the splendor of Carmel and Sharon (Isaiah 35:2).

Lebanon stands out for the stately strength of her cedars. Cedars play a very important role in the Old Testament. Solomon spoke of them as trees of importance (1 Kings 4:33). The psalmist tells us the Lord himself planted the cedars of Lebanon: "The trees of the Lord are well watered, the cedars of Lebanon that he planted" (Psalm 104:16).

In Zechariah, the fall of the glorious people of God is likened to a fire devouring the great trees of Lebanon:

Open your doors, O Lebanon, so that fire may devour your cedars! Wail, O pine tree, for the cedar has fallen; the stately trees are ruined! Wail, oaks of Bashan; the dense forest has been cut down! (11:1, 2).

These trees would grow to an impressive height of over 100 feet and circumference of 40 to 60 feet. Stately and glorious, they were used for many different purposes. The great thing about them was the fact they had so much resin in them and they were very resistant to rot and insects. These majestic cedars were prominent, useful and tough, and they were prized and cared for by the Lord himself.

God says He is willing to do the same in the life of those who feel they are in a deserted place. He is willing to come alongside, water you with His glory and make something wonderful out of your life! When God moves in your life, you won't recognize yourself. Right now, you may feel like a weed growing in desert sand, but when God gets through moving in your life, you will be like a cedar, planted by the rivers of water.

The Lord also said He would give you the "splendor of Carmel and Sharon." Carmel refers to the great mountain and literally means "a garden with fruit trees." It provides its inhabitants with an abundance not found in other areas of the land. When the flowers are in full bloom, Carmel is said to be like a multicolored blanket, unrivaled in spectacular beauty.

Sharon is a plain at the base of Carmel that consists of rolling hills covered with deep, rich soil. It is famous for its olives, and its orange groves are world-renowned.

Those don't sound like deserted places to me. Instead, they sound like a paradise. God is saying He will take your deserted places and turn them into great areas of prosperity. He can move in the most hostile environment imaginable and make it a rapturous Eden.

Understanding His awesome power to bring life and vitality into hostile environments, we need to press in to His presence and allow Him to rain His glory on us. No matter what you are going through, don't give up. No matter how bad things are right now, hold on. God knows how to show up in your deserted places and make them bloom like a rose!

What kind of deserted places can God move in?

A Place of Deserted Prayers

Some of us know all too well what this desert looks like. We prayed at one time, asking the Lord for something great. We believed for a mighty answer from God. Perhaps it was for a loved one's salvation. It could have been for healing to come into someone's life. It might even have been for a real move of God in your own life. You thought the answer was coming. You hoped it was coming. But it didn't.

Now, over a period of time, you have deserted the prayer—placed it on the shelf and decided it just isn't worth the effort any longer. Sometimes we find ourselves in the same deserted place as did Zechariah, the father of John the Baptist.

The time had come for Zechariah to offer incense upon the altar to God. While everyone else was outside praying, he was inside, worshiping the Lord. Suddenly, he looked over in the corner and saw an angel. Most of us would have had the same reaction as he did at that moment. Like him, we would have been scared to death.

> Then an angel of the Lord appeared to him, standing at the right side of the altar of incense. When Zechariah saw him, he was startled and was gripped with fear. But the angel said to him: "Do not be afraid, Zechariah; your prayer has been heard. Your wife Elizabeth will bear you a son, and you are to give him the name John" (Luke 1:11-13).

This godly man and his wife had been praying for the gift of a son. However, I think they had deserted the request. Over the years, God had closed the womb of Elizabeth. I know they had prayed, but verse 18 gives more insight: "Zechariah asked the angel, 'How can I be sure of this? I am an old man and my wife is well along in years.'"

Zechariah had lost the faith to believe God was going to do something. He once had faith. If you don't have a root of faith, there is no way you are going to pray for something year after year. Zechariah's faith had been deserted. He had put his prayer on the sideline. He had neglected and forgotten the request that had been urgent. In his youth, this request was foremost in his life and his prayer for a son had consumed him. But as time passed, both he and Elizabeth grew accustomed to living alone. Somewhere along the way, they deserted their prayer for a child.

That's exactly where some of us are right now. In the springtime of our Christian experience, we dared to pray for great things. Some of our prayers were answered, some weren't. Those things we were desperate about in the beginning gradually lost their luster and importance.

- We started thinking, Well, maybe it just isn't God's will for them to be saved.

- We grew accustomed to living a substandard Christian life and settled into a pattern of defeat.

- We decided the gifts of the Spirit weren't for us and gave up on the dream of being used by the Lord.

- We reached a faulty conclusion that it was always going to be the other person, the other church, that was going to experience a mighty move of God.

- Somewhere along the way we deserted our prayer for the greater things of God and settled for the good.

Never forget that God can show up and move mightily in prayers you have deserted. He can work wonders in places you thought were too dry, too hard, too dead, too difficult. Keep seeking His face—one day you may be going through your regular duties and the Lord will show up! The answer to that prayer you prayed long ago will come walking in the door.

Deserted Dreams and Visions

Many of us live with a faint remembrance of what we once thought God would make of us. We look back, with a certain wistfulness, on those days when we had a vision of doing something great for God. Many churches are operating today without a vision of doing something wonderful for God. For those churches, dreams and visions have been replaced by the weekly drudgery of keeping the doors open and bills paid. Many believers simply live from week to week, hoping to keep it together until Jesus comes. For some of us, He had better come in a hurry!

Sadly, many of us live a mediocre Christian existence— a series of "I'm sorry, Lord," followed by failure after failure and the hope that Jesus will understand. The strength and vitality of victorious Christian living is gone.

That vision, that dream, that goal of being somebody for Christ has been forgotten. Somewhere along our journey, we got tired, or hurt, or disappointed in someone. Some pastor let us down. Some favorite Christian went bad. Someone in the church offended us. Allowing that to dominate us, our spiritual spunk and stamina waned and we lost our visionary edge. Now, we are merely holding the fort until Jesus comes.

We need to ask these questions: "Has anyone in the Bible ever been in this place? Did God move in his or her life?" The answer comes screaming back at us from the pages of God's Word, "Yes!" Does a man named David ring a bell? Listen to his woeful cry.

But David thought to himself, "One of these days I will be destroyed by the hand of Saul. The best thing I can do is to escape to the land of the Philistines. Then Saul will give up searching for me anywhere in Israel, and I will slip out of his hand" (1 Samuel 27:1).

David had already demonstrated great vision and passion for God as well as an uncanny anointing from on high.

- He had killed the lion, bear, and the Philistine.

- He had been anointed future king of Israel.

- He had spared Saul's life.

- He had heard the inspired words of Samuel.

But he lost his sense of spiritual bearing, convinced he would never rise above his circumstances to become what God declared him to be. Fear and depression seized his dream. It would not be long before he was acting like everything but what he was—a king.

That strikes uncomfortably close to home. How many of us have given up on our vision and dream of becoming a mighty man or woman of God and have stopped acting like the very people we are—children of the King of kings?

David didn't understand it, but God was going to show up and fulfill his deserted dream. It would be said of him, "David reigns in Jerusalem." Had I been there and known then what I know now, I could have said, "David, don't let go of the vision. Don't lose the dream. God will show up and move in your life!"

Unfortunately, we aren't given that privilege of fore-knowledge. We have to look forward in faith. We have to press through the attacks of the Enemy and trust God to show up in our time of need.

Child of God, you may have deserted your vision of blessing and power and become surrounded by want and weakness. God can show up and transform your desert into a lush paradise. Struggling lamb of God, your dream of living in victory may have been deserted and replaced by an empty and arid experience which brings no joy or contentment. God can show up and make you flourish in your desert.

Mother, the dream of your children and grandchildren serving God may be languishing like a rain-starved fruit on the vine. God can move in your desert and cause life to spring forth. As you read this, your family may be in the middle of a tough time. The vision of your family bound in unity and love may have been shattered by infidelity or a tragedy. The God we serve can cause your love to flourish like the cedars on the hillsides of Lebanon. He can transform the pain of your circumstance into rapturous joy.

It's never too late with God. Your situation is not so far gone that God cannot bring His power and might into your life. Your church is not so dead that God cannot rekindle the vision that once propelled it into the harvest field. The visions and dreams that once captivated hearts can live again. A fresh touch of His glory will cause them to rise up and live once more.

The Place of Deserted Commitment

Perhaps the most amazing place God will show up and make His presence known is in the midst of a deserted commitment. That is the place where many of us dwell today. Our desert, our wilderness, is a place of our own making. We once followed hard after God, now we only catch fleeting glimpses of Him. At one time our hearts were filled with passion for the Lord, now we get by with perfunctory church attendance. The joy that once characterized our walk with Christ has evaporated into a dull and monotonous routine of hoping we can live right just long enough to escape hell and enter heaven.

It doesn't have to be that way. God can move even in a life like that. He did it for a man named Samson. His is one of the most famous stories in all the Bible. Toying with temptation, he eventually fell. As will happen with all of us, he played with fire once too often and wound up getting burned. Look at him after the tragic tale is played out:

> Now the temple was crowded with men and women; all the rulers of the Philistines were there, and on the roof were about three thousand men and women watching Samson perform. Then Samson prayed to the Lord, "O Sovereign Lord, remember me. O God, please strengthen me just once more, and let me with one blow get revenge on the Philistines for my two eyes." Then Samson reached toward the two central pillars on which the temple stood. Bracing himself against them, his right hand on the one and his left hand on the other, Samson said, "Let me die with the Philistines!" Then he pushed with all his might, and down came the temple on the rulers and all the people in it. Thus he killed many more when he died than while he lived (Judges 16:27-30).

He had deserted his commitment, but God still had something in store for Him. He had made a royal mess out of his life, but God cared enough to show up when the man needed His help. That's how faithful our God is. We renege on our commitment, we abandon our loyalty, and what does God do? He comes to our side when we call on His name.

No doubt some of us have made many commitments to the Lord. We have stated many times how we will serve Him, only to fail at the last moment. For this we can be profoundly thankful—our heavenly Father is not like us!

The best news in the world is that when we blow it, make a mess of things, really wreck our lives, God is still right there to help us. Sure, we will have to pay a price (Samson had to give up his eyesight and have his life cut short), but God will give us the grace we need in our most desperate hour. Remember this—in your worst time, even when you have walked away from God, He will be right there waiting when you call on His name!

Has your commitment to pray been deserted? He will be right there for you if you will call on His name. Has your commitment to read His Word waned? He is there, waiting for you. Has your commitment for spiritual growth turned into a barren desert? He will be right there and give you abundant life. Just call on His name. He will show up. He will move in your life again. He will make His mighty presence known once more. All you have to do is call on Jesus, He will be right there.

This is not a smoke screen or a hyped-up, hoped-for thing. Consider the lasting implications of this great promise: "The burning sand will become a pool, the thirsty ground bubbling springs" (Isaiah 35:7).

The term *burning sand* in Hebrew means a mirage. It is something that allures thirsty travelers with the promise of water, only to lead them to disaster. It never satisfies or fulfills. It only taunts and mocks those who come near. In fact, the closer you get, the hazier the reality becomes.

God's promise is nothing like that. It holds up under scrutiny. His presence is water in a dry land. His presence is a stream in the desert. We can know that when we dare to call on the Lord and trust in His name, He delivers. Why not open up the desert of your life today and let Him flood you with His presence? You will begin to bloom like a rose.

<h1 style="text-align:center">7</h1>

God Will Move in Dead Places

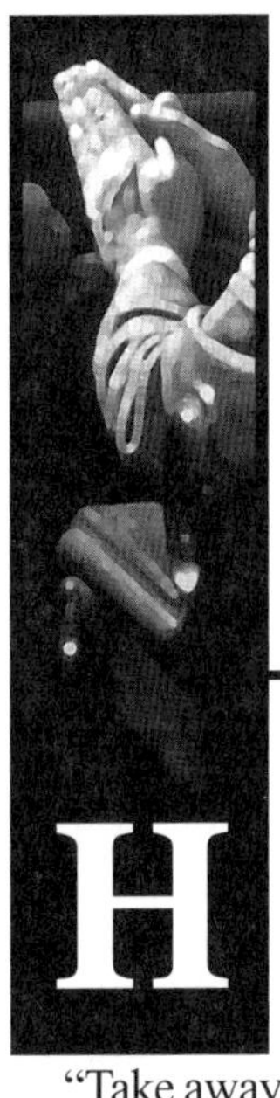

He asked me, "Son of man, can these bones live?" I said, "O Sovereign Lord, you alone know" (Ezekiel 37:3).

"Take away the stone," he said. "But, Lord," said Martha, the sister of the dead man, "by this time there is a bad odor, for he has been there four days" (John 11:39).

One of the hardest things for us to believe is that God can move in something dead and make it live again. For instance, when the Lord spoke to Ezekiel, He asked the prophet a question, "Zeke, can these bones live again?"

To Ezekiel's credit, he didn't try an end run on God— he simply spoke what was in his heart. "God, I don't know. The only one who knows that answer is You."

I am sure Ezekiel had a high regard for God's ability and faith in God's power. If you take the time to read the first chapter of the book bearing his name, you understand this: The man caught a vision of the Almighty like few have, before or since. Still, when confronted with the grim specter of death, he wasn't sure there was any way God could do anything.

Mary and Martha faced the same dilemma. Death had taken their beloved Lazarus away. When Jesus finally arrived, they were not at all convinced there was anything that could be done about the situation, although they were acutely aware of the power of the Lord to do awesome things. Witness the testimony of Mary:

> When Mary reached the place where Jesus was and saw him, she fell at his feet and said, "Lord, if you had been here, my brother would not have died" (John 11:32).

She knew Jesus had the power to heal her brother, but death was an entirely different matter in her mind. When the Prince of Life told them to move the stone blocking the entrance to the grave of Lazarus, Martha chided Him, telling Him that the odor from decomposition would be strong. Rolling the stone away seemed to be a senseless and tasteless thing to do.

Why would Ezekiel and Mary, two people who knew about the power of God, have this sagging faith when it came to the ability of God to overcome death? Do you think they struggled then, as we struggle today, with the ability of God to act powerfully when death has come? We can do many things today they could not do in Biblical days. We can water deserts and make them bloom. We can move great mountains with explosives and heavy machinery. We can even stave off some diseases and extend life. But death? We still can't do anything about death.

Here's where our problem lies: we have framed God in our image. Because we can't do anything about death, we assume God can't do anything either.

Nothing could be further from the truth. We forget the wonderful reality of God's ability to reach into death and pull life right back. He can take what is dead and make it live again.

Naturally, when death comes to our physical bodies, we bury them and wait for the resurrection. Though it may seem death has won, the day will come when the universal curse of death will be defeated. I love what Jesus said:

> "Do not be amazed at this, for a time is coming when all who are in their graves will hear his voice and come out—those who have done good will rise to live, and those who have done evil will rise to be condemned" (John 5:28, 29).

I long for that day, and you can count on the fact that it's coming. Every graveyard containing the body of a believer will one day be invaded by the presence of the Almighty. In one glorious moment, the Savior will call together all mankind who love His appearing and we will shout, "Death, where is your sting? Grave, where is your victory?"

But what about today? What about a marriage that is dead? What about a future that is dead? What about a relationship between parents and children that is dead? What about a church that is dead? How about a relationship with God that is dead? Is it possible for God to move there? Is it possible for God to move in *my* life, even though my hopes and dreams are dead?

I want to go one step beyond Ezekiel and Mary and answer, "Yes! It is possible! With God, *all* things are possible!"

As we examine these two incidents, I see some glaring similarities. Separated by centuries, these two events bear startling testimony to the power of God to move in the midst of the most daunting situations. We clearly see the ability of God and His power to reverse the very things that leave men powerless.

Extreme Circumstances

In both cases, God moved into a place where death had reigned supreme. Dire circumstances dominated the landscape. The descriptions of the two situations vary in detail, but both point to the same conclusion: nothing could be done!

> He led me back and forth among them, and I saw a great many bones on the floor of the valley, bones that were very dry (Ezekiel 37:2).

Similarly, Jesus found that Lazarus had been in the tomb for four days (see John 11:17).

First, Ezekiel sees bones that are "very dry." The Hebrew means "vehemently dried up." Before him is a pile of bones that have been there long enough for the sun and wind to have their devastating effect. These individuals, whoever they once were, had been dead for a long time.

Lazarus, on the other hand, had been in the tomb for four days. When you have been buried for four days, you are dead—graveyard dead! He had been in the tomb for so long that the natural decay in his body had started.

In both cases, men are placed beyond the extremity of their ability to change anything. About all you could do for the bones in the desert was gather them and give them some type of proper burial. And about all you could do for Lazarus was commemorate his life and visit the tomb. Apart from that, men were at a loss.

Isn't it wonderful to note that our extremity is God's opportunity? When we reach the end of our ability to do anything, God is ready to demonstrate His ability to make a difference.

Consider the story of Jeannie Raborg as told in R.T. Kendall's wonderful book, *When God Shows Up*. Jeannie was raised in a Presbyterian home. When she was 8 years old, she was sent to a summer camp for girls. One night, sitting around the campfire, the counselor told the girls to throw a pinecone into the fire and make a wish. Jeannie did, and her wish was simple. "God," she said, "if You are really there, I'd like to know You." That was it. No bells. No whistles.

Jeannie went on to the university and became a teacher. According to her story, one day a student brought a question up to her desk. The next thing she remembered, she was in the hospital. After struggling and going from bad to worse, Jeannie eventually had to be admitted to a secure mental hospital. She had suffered a complete nervous breakdown. As the attendants took her behind the iron door to lock her away, she pleaded with her husband, "Please, don't do this to me!" With tears flowing down his face he responded, "I don't know anything else to do."

Four years later, an evangelist came to the town where Jeannie's mother lived. At one of the services, she went to the altar for prayer. She told the evangelist, Paul Cain, of her daughter's need. Cain felt the Lord leading him and told her he would pray for her daughter. Finding out where Jeannie was being held, he prepared to make the 500-mile trip. He called the family and gave them this word: "Tell your grandmother and your father that your mother will be home in three days—and she will be well."

The family didn't believe it. They had heard that kind of false promise before. Jeannie was simply too far gone for anything to be done for her.

Making his way to the hospital, Cain finally found Jeannie. She was licking envelopes, the only activity her drug-induced state would allow. When he told Jeannie he was there to pray for her, she said, "There is no hope for me." God's man responded, "Ah, the Lord says to you in Isaiah 41:10: 'Fear not, for I am with you; be not dismayed'" (*NKJV*).

Jeannie perked up and told him that was the one verse of Scripture she had leaned on for years. Then Cain said, "I really don't understand this, but the Lord wants me to tell you that He has never forgotten the 8-year-old girl who threw the pinecone into the fire and said she wanted to know Him personally."

Cain prayed for this extreme case no one could help. The next day the psychiatrist came in and asked Jeannie, "What has happened to you?" She said, "I'm healed and I want to go home." He said, "You are not going home." He started a series of tests and three days later, Jeannie went home![1]

That was over 20 years ago, and she has been well ever since. How could this happen? It's simple—when we reach the end of our ability, we are only beginning to experience the power of the Almighty.

- A man can be sick for 38 years, but that doesn't mean he cannot be healed.

- A woman can be bound by Satan for 18 years, but that doesn't mean she can't be set free.

- A man can be so demonically empowered that the strongest chains of men cannot hold him, but that doesn't mean he is too far gone for God.

- A woman may have spent her last dime on doctors, but that doesn't mean the Great Physician cannot show up and take over the case.

- Your marriage may appear so far gone there is no hope, but the Wonderful Counselor is still able.

- Your financial condition may seem unsalvageable, but the Great Provider is still around.

- Your disease may be untreatable by man, but there is still a God who can do as He pleases.

When you have reached the end, congratulations. You are about to venture into the exclusive domain of the Almighty.

Willing to Do Our Part

As can be seen in the cases of both Ezekiel and Lazarus, before God moved in the dead places, those standing around had to do something at the command of the Lord.

Then he said to me, "Prophesy to these bones and say to them, 'Dry bones, hear the word of the Lord!'" (Ezekiel 37:4).

"Take away the stone," he said. "But, Lord," said Martha, the sister of the dead man, "by this time there is a bad odor, for he has been there four days" (John 11:39).

Ezekiel had to prophesy, or speak the word of God, to a bunch of dried-up bones. Martha had to be quiet and allow men to heave a large stone from the entrance of a tomb. In both cases, someone had to be willing to do what God said. This is where the majority of us lose out on having God do the miraculous in our dead places. God is ready to do something. He speaks to us about our part, but what He demands is too exacting, and we fail to follow through. Consequently, we stand around and wonder why God isn't moving in our lives like we hear He can. The problem isn't God—it's us!

When you think about it, Ezekiel looked like an idiot standing out there in the hot sun, preaching to a bunch of bones. One night, a fellowship group of 40 or so adults from my church gathered at a rib joint in Mobile called Dreamland.

That night the whole group ate ribs (what I call "pigcicles" because any sick child will tell you how good a Popsicle is when you don't feel good). There were bones everywhere. And we were not alone. There were many others present doing the same thing. I thought about Ezekiel. Can you imagine how silly, how utterly absurd, you would look if someone caught you standing out by the dumpster of that restaurant, calling out to a bunch of pig bones, "Live!"? They would be calling for the guys in the white suits to put you in a straitjacket.

Ezekiel had to be willing to do something absurd, something out of the ordinary. He had to be willing to do something unquestionably ridiculous to witness God moving in a dead place. There was no room for compromise. It was a risk he had to take.

By the same measure, Martha and those around her had to risk appearing ghoulish and morbidly bizarre in order to see the Lord move in their dead place. Public opinion would have branded them "grave robbers," had something miraculous not transpired. Additionally, their religion would have labeled them unclean zealots, had Lazarus not come forth.

In both situations, those who were around during the move of God had to be willing to do something everyone else considered foolish. When will we ever learn that the ways of God are diametrically opposed to the ways of man?

> "For my thoughts are not your thoughts, neither are your ways my ways," declares the Lord. "As the heavens are higher than the earth, so are my ways higher than your ways and my thoughts than your thoughts" (Isaiah 55:8, 9).

Many of us are like Naaman, a man with a great need—a dead spot in his life. Actually, he had leprosy that ate away at him every day. When the time came that God was willing to revive the dead place in his life, he was called on to do something that, from the human standpoint, was foolish. When he heard from the prophet the deed he was to do in order to see God move in his life, it was just too much for his pride.

> Elisha sent a messenger to say to him, "Go, wash yourself seven times in the Jordan, and your flesh will be

restored and you will be cleansed." But Naaman went away angry and said, "I thought that he would surely come out to me and stand and call on the name of the Lord his God, wave his hand over the spot and cure me of my leprosy. Are not Abana and Pharpar, the rivers of Damascus, better than any of the waters of Israel? Couldn't I wash in them and be cleansed?" So he turned and went off in a rage (2 Kings 5:10-12).

Seven dips in the Jordan . . . doesn't sound like too much to me to be healed of a lifelong disease, but it struck a nerve in Naaman, ruffling his pride. This is precisely why most of us don't see much of the glory of God in our lives. We are dead and decaying on the inside, but so full of pride that we shrink back when the Lord calls on us to do something out of the ordinary, like speaking to dry bones or rolling the stone away from a stinking cave.

Like Naaman, we go off in a rage. "How dare they call on me to do that!" is our usual response. "Who do they think they are?" is another well-worn statement from someone whose pride has been insulted by a person who has heard from the Lord. Here's another pet favorite, "Don't they know who I am?" And off we go, in a huff, still dying on the inside.

- Naaman wanted the televangelist method of healing. "Come out, wave your hands over me, make it all go away." God wanted to use the prayer-closet method.

- Naaman wanted the spectacular out of a sense of pride. He was from the land of "clean water." He deserved it! God was willing to do it because a slave girl and a prophet heard His word.

- Naaman wanted the other guy to "do it all." Note his incensed attitude that Elisha didn't come to him, wave his hand over him, call on his, that is, Elisha's god. But God wanted Naaman to know he had a part to do as well.

So many of us are willing for God to do something, just as long as we don't have to go out on a limb . . . just as long as we don't risk anything . . . just as long as it won't bring any bad repercussions on us.

What slow learners we are. God never used anyone, never moved in the life of anyone, who wasn't willing to lay it all on the line and take a risk.

In 1521, the church was a very dangerous place. If you disagreed with certain people, it bought you a quick one-way ticket to see Jesus. A monk named Martin Luther decided it was worth the risk. He published some tracts that flew in the face of the hierarchy of the church. When called to answer for his insolence, he was pushed to recant what he had written. Up against the wall, he told them he would recant, but only if they could find anything in his statement contrary to the Word of God. In a moment of risk, he then stated, "But if not, here I stand. I can do no other. God help me. Amen."

Because he was willing to take the risk, the world was forever changed. All because one man was willing to follow God, even when it meant possible disaster in his life.

You and I will never see the hand of God move if we are watching from the safety of the sideline. We will never experience God's life-giving power in our dead spots unless we are willing to become fools for Christ's sake. It's time we throw off the two oppressing weights that cause us to stumble before a great move of God: the fear of men's opinion and our feebleness to pursue the Almighty.

Fear is killing us. Pentecostals and Charismatics are becoming afraid of what the "world" has to say about us. We have grown sensitive to the criticisms of those who would stifle a move of God, and we strive to make everything in the Kingdom palatable to those who do not understand Kingdom dynamics.

Feebleness is eating our lives away. We make half-hearted, wimpy attempts to follow the leadership of the Holy Spirit, only to be distracted by the latest new theological distraction or political argument.

Once again, it is time for us to take on the courage of Ezekiel and speak to the dead spots in our lives—dead marriages, dead relationships, dead hopes, dead dreams, dead financial situations, dead emotional lives—and tell them to live in the name of the Prince of Life! It's time for someone, somewhere, to roll the stone from the grave of a dead church and trust the promise of Jesus that it can live again.

God's Timing

Just when we think we have God figured out and have a good grasp on what He is doing, He will let us know we aren't nearly as clever as we think. He goes much deeper and takes more time than we imagine.

Note the progression in Ezekiel's mighty miracle:

Then he said to me, "Prophesy to these bones and say to them, 'Dry bones, hear the word of the Lord! This is what the Sovereign Lord says to these bones: I will make breath enter you, and you will come to life. I will attach tendons to you and make flesh come upon you and cover you with skin; I will put breath in you, and you will come to life. Then you will know that I am the Lord.'" So I prophesied as I was commanded. And as I was prophesying, there was a noise, a rattling sound, and the bones came together, bone to bone. I looked, and tendons and flesh appeared on them and skin covered them, but there was no breath in them. Then he said to me, "Prophesy to the breath; prophesy, son of man, and say to it, 'This is what the Sovereign Lord says: Come from the four winds, O breath, and breathe into these slain, that they may live.'" So I prophesied as he commanded me, and breath entered them; they came to life and stood up on their feet—a vast army. Then he said to me: "Son of man, these bones are the whole house of Israel. They say, 'Our bones are dried up and our hope is gone; we are cut off.' Therefore prophesy and say to them: 'This is what the Sovereign Lord says: O my people, I am going to open your graves and bring you up from them; I will bring you back to the land of Israel. Then you, my people, will know that I am the Lord, when I open your graves and bring you up from them. I will put my Spirit in you and you will live, and I will settle you in your own land. Then you will know that I the Lord have spoken, and I have done it, declares the Lord'" (Ezekiel 37:4-14).

When Ezekiel spoke the word of the Lord, something amazing happened. Bones started jumping up and joining each other. Next, tendons came, then flesh, then skin. Suddenly, there was a mighty army of breathless corpses standing there. That is a mighty miracle, but that's not all God had planned. There was more—with God, there is always more.

He spoke again and God blew breath into the lifeless bodies. Life came into death and suddenly there was a mighty army standing there. It took more than one touch, more than one prophecy, more than one prayer meeting, but God did something breathtaking. Ezekiel could have prematurely gone out and started his "Bone-to-Bone Seminar" and made a fortune, but God wanted to do more. Ezekiel had to stay and wait for God to do more.

Next, God thundered the real reason for all this fuss. He told Ezekiel He was going to visit Israel's dead places and do a mighty work.

> "Therefore prophesy and say to them: 'This is what the Sovereign Lord says: O my people, I am going to open your graves and bring you up from them; I will bring you back to the land of Israel'" (v. 12).

The Lord told of His plans to swing by the graveyards of dead hopes and dreams. He was going to make a visit to the graveyards of dead relationships and cause them to live again.

Here's the message we need to hear and take to heart today: God will raise up our dead aspirations in newness of life. What He started, He will complete.

Nowhere is this seen in a clearer light than with Lazarus. I love the picture John paints for us:

> When he had said this, Jesus called in a loud voice, "Lazarus, come out!" The dead man came out, his hands

and feet wrapped with strips of linen, and a cloth around his face. Jesus said to them, "Take off the grave clothes and let him go" (John 11:43, 44).

When Jesus called out to the dead man, he came out of the grave. What a mighty miracle! What a demonstration of our Lord's power to move in the dead places. But wait . . . there was something we all need to notice in this joyous scene. It's almost humorous—like a funeral when nothing is supposed to be funny, but everything is. Lazarus was bound up tighter than bark on a tree. He was literally jumping up and down like a pogo stick in order to get out of that grave.

As soon as Lazarus died, according to the custom of the day, the oldest son, or the next of kin, would go in and close the eyes. Following that, the jaws would be bound with cord to keep the mouth shut. The body would then be wrapped with rolls of clean cloth and pounds of spices and herbs inserted to keep the smell to a minimum. Lazarus came out of that tomb like a mummy with his mouth tied shut.

God had done a great work, but there was more to be done. The man had to be loosed and set free so he could tell the wondrous works of Jesus.

Jesus could have caused the wrappings to fall off. He could have caused Lazarus to come out of the grave wearing the finest suit available in the time. After all, if you can call a man back from the dead after four days, what are a few bandages to you? Why didn't the Lord just make Lazarus appear in an Armani suit? I think Jesus wanted us to see the importance of our involvement and patience.

Don't limit the Lord's ability to move in the dead places that have haunted your life for years. Wait on the Lord with full assurance of His power and willingness to move in your life. When He shows up, life will overtake death, and joy will trample sorrow into the ground.

8

God Will Move in Demonic Places

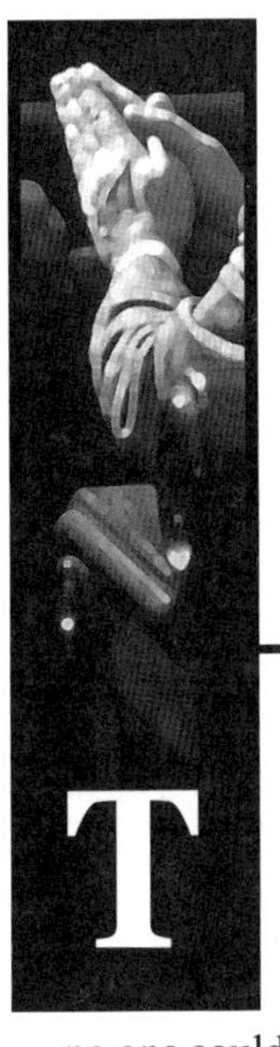

hey went across the lake to the region of the Gerasenes. When Jesus got out of the boat, a man with an evil spirit came from the tombs to meet him. This man lived in the tombs, and no one could bind him any more, not even with a chain. He had often been chained hand and foot, but he tore the chains apart and broke the irons on his feet. No one was strong enough to subdue him. Night and day among the tombs and in the hills he would cry out among the tombs in the hills, and cut himself with stones. When he saw Jesus from a distance, he ran and fell on his knees in front of him. He shouted at the top of his voice, "What do you want with me, Jesus, Son of the Most High God? Swear to God that you won't torture me!" For Jesus had said to him, "Come out of this man, you evil spirit!" Then Jesus asked him, "What is your name?" "My name is Legion," he replied, "for we are many." And he begged Jesus again and again not to send them out of the area. A large herd of pigs was feeding on the nearby hillside. The demons begged Jesus,

"Send us among the pigs; allow us to go into them." He gave them permission, and the evil spirits came out and went into the pigs. The herd, about two thousand in number, rushed down the steep bank into the lake and were drowned (Mark 5:1-13).

Do we really believe God can move in the territory of Satan and his demonic forces? Many of us have given up hope of God's might and power moving in the demonic areas around us. We are selling God short and giving Satan far too much credit. Our Lord can walk right into the most demon-infested spot and restore what has been destroyed. Thank God, Jesus is Lord of all things, and that includes the hosts of demonic powers running loose in the earth today.

Right up front, we need to speak to the issue of demons. As far as I can tell, C.S. Lewis, in his classic book *The Screwtape Letters,* hit the nail on the head:

> There are two equal and opposite errors into which our race can fall about the devils. One is to disbelieve in their existence. The other is to believe, and to feel an excessive and unhealthy interest in them. They themselves are equally pleased by both errors and hail a materialist and a magician with the same delight.[1]

Many, on one hand, seek for nothing but a natural cause for all evil. If someone does something dastardly and horrible, it must have, at its genesis, a natural cause. Blinded to anything spiritual, the natural man must search, often in vain, for the reason behind the madness of our age.

On the other hand, there are those in the religious cast who go to the opposite extreme. They, in the well-worn bromide, find a demon behind every bush. In their desire to find the reason for the madness of men, demons cause it all. If you sneeze, a demon tickled your nose. If you have a headache, a demon is squeezing your head. I concur with Kent Hughes, "If Satan cannot pull you down, he will just as happily push you overboard."[2]

Setting the two extremes aside, anyone who accepts the Bible at face value must concede the existence and diabolical working of evil spirits, those things we call demons. They are under the orders of Satan himself and are sent to carry out his pernicious plans. At times we encounter them in graphic gore, as in the case of a man named David Berkowitz, otherwise known as the "Son of Sam" killer.

According to his own testimony from prison (from which he will never emerge alive), he was tormented as a child. Disruptive and mean, he had trouble in school and had to be physically restrained. Over time, his obsessive interest in the occult and horror movies made him vulnerable to the attack of demonic powers. At age 22, David went over the edge and became the villain we know as "Son of Sam." For a period of about one year, he terrorized New York. Using a powerful handgun, he shot individuals at random, killing six and injuring many more. During the height of the manhunt for this murderous monster, David sent a couple of taunting letters to the police, proving the torment of this man's soul:

Dear Captain Joseph Borrelli,
I am deeply hurt by your calling me a woman hater. I am not. But I am a monster. I am the "Son of Sam." I am a little brat. When the father of Sam gets drunk, he gets mean. He beats his family. Sometimes he ties me up to

the back of the house. Other times he locks me in the garage. Sam loves to drink blood. "Go out and kill," commands father Sam. "Behind our house is some rest. Mostly young . . . raped and slaughtered . . . their blood drained . . . just bones now." Papa Sam keeps me locked in the attic too. I can't get out, but I look out the attic window and watch the world go by.

I feel like an outsider. I am on a different wavelength than everybody else—programmed to kill. However, to stop me you must kill me. Attention all police: Shoot me first—shoot to kill, or else keep out of my way or you will die!

Papa Sam is old now. He needs some blood to preserve his youth. He has had too many heart attacks. "Ugh, me hoot, it hurts, sonny boy!"

I miss my pretty princess most of all. She's resting in our ladies house. But I'll see her soon. I am the "Monster"—"Beelzebub"—the chubby behemoth. I love to hunt. Prowling the streets looking for fair game . . . tasty meat. The women of Queens are prettiest of all. It must be the water they drink. I live for the hunt—my life. Blood for Papa.

Mr. Borrelli, sir, I don't want to kill anymore. No sir, no more, but I must "honor thy father." I want to make love to the world. I love people. I don't belong on earth. Return me to yahoos.

To the people of Queens, I love you. And I want to wish all of you a happy Easter. My God bless you in this life and the next.[3]

(Spelling changes made for clarity)

Later, another letter appeared from David:

Hello from the cracks in the sidewalks of NYC and from the ants that dwell in those cracks and feed in the dried blood of the dead that has settled into the cracks.

Hello from the gutters of NYC which is filled with dog manure, vomit, stale wine, urine and blood. Hello from the sewers of NYC which swallow up these delicacies when they are washed away by the sweeper trucks.

Don't think because you haven't heard [from me] for a while that I went to sleep. No, rather, I am still here. Like a spirit roaming the night. Thirsty, hungry, seldom stopping to rest; anxious to please Sam.

Sam's a thirsty lad. He won't let me stop killing until he gets his fill of blood. Tell me, Jim, what will you have for July 29? You can forget about me if you want to because I don't care for publicity. However, you must not forget Donna Lauria, and you cannot let the people forget her either. She was a very sweet girl. [Donna Lauria was the first victim of the Son of Sam.]

Not knowing what the future holds, I shall say farewell and I will see you at the next job? Or should I say you will see my handiwork at the next job? Remember Ms. Lauria. Thank you.

In their blood and from the gutter . . . "Sam's" creation.[4]

The world looks for a genetic cause, or an environmental cause, of such horrific behavior. Perhaps there is.

However, looking beyond what men can see, there is the overwhelming image of Satan at work. Much like the man Jesus met that day on the lakeshore, David Berkowitz was terribly driven by powerful demon forces.

Can God move in a place as demonically fortified as the heart of David Berkowitz? Is there hope for such a hopeless situation? Well, if Jesus is who we say He is—indeed, if Jesus has the power and authority He professes to possess—I must shout loud and long, "Yes, God can move even in demonic places and set men free!"

Hidden Strongholds

One place where demonic people can be found is at church. That's right, church! Did you know it is possible for someone totally possessed of the devil to hang out in church and not even be noticed? According to the Bible, it happens.

They went to Capernaum, and when the Sabbath came, Jesus went into the synagogue and began to teach. The people were amazed at his teaching, because he taught them as one who had authority, not as the teachers of the law. Just then a man in their synagogue who was possessed by an evil spirit cried out, "What do you want with us, Jesus of Nazareth? Have you come to destroy us? I know who you are—the Holy One of God!" "Be quiet!" said Jesus sternly. "Come out of him!" The evil spirit shook the man violently and came out of him with a shriek. The people were all so amazed that they asked each other, "What is this? A new teaching—and with authority! He even gives orders to evil spirits and they obey him." News about him spread quickly over the whole region of Galilee (Mark 1:21-28).

Here's a man in church who is driven by demons. He remains hidden until a move of God comes along and reveals who he really is. That's the nature of the kingdom of darkness: Hide in the shadows; work in the obscure; don't be blatant with your rebellion.

Sin—the breeding ground of demonic activity—works in this same fashion. We come to church with our sinful thoughts, actions and desires pretty much covered up— until a move of the Holy Spirit comes along and exposes us.

Rest assured, Satan and his entire kingdom will rear their heads when the Holy Spirit begins to move. It may come in the form of rebellion that says, "I don't like that and I won't have any part of it." It may arise in the form of religion that says, "It has never been done that way before, so it can't be of God." It may stick out as indifference that says, "Oh well, that's fine for them, but I don't want to get involved." But when the Spirit of the Lord shows up, you can count on the activity of demons to increase.

Does that mean Jesus can't move in an area where demons influence people? Not at all. Jesus can move in any place He wants to move. He can march into a nest of demons and send them scattering like pins hit by a bowling ball. When He encountered this demon in the church-going man, He sternly told the evil spirit, "Be quiet and come out of him!" There was no argument. No hassle. No bargaining. Just the simple obedience of a lesser power to a greater power.

This is a good place to point something out: a sincere believer—always praying, repenting, living in victory, feeding on the Word, fellowshipping in church—has nothing to fear from the demons that serve Satan! The world is powerless against them, but we are not of this world.

- We have the Son of God praying for us.

- We have the Holy Spirit sealing us.

- We have the Spirit of God living inside us.

- We have the angels of heaven protecting us.

- We have the Word of God as a weapon.

- We have praise that will silence the mouth of the Enemy.

- We have the promise that no weapon formed against us will prosper.

- We have the promise that the One inside us is greater than the one in the world.

We don't need to fear demons. We can refuse to be blinded by the Hollywood image of some demonic being coming against us and overwhelming us. If we are washed in the blood of the Lamb and sealed by the Spirit of God, they will hate us, attack us, tempt us, harass us—but they can't overcome us!

Hopeless Situations

The man we encountered at the tombs earlier epitomizes the hopelessness associated with Satan and his kingdom. Take a look at him once more.

- He lived in the tombs among rotting corpses with the maggots, worms, rats, and other vermin that feasted on dead and decaying flesh.

- He was not able to be restrained. When they put chains on him, some Herculean strength would flow through his body and he would break them.

- Night and day he howled in misery.

- He was suicidal, constantly cutting himself with stones.

- The people had tried every conceivable means of making him better, but nothing worked. He was hopeless.

Do you ever feel powerless? I do. Quite often I do. When I see the working of Satan's kingdom on the lives of people around me, I sense some of the powerlessness and hopelessness that must have pervaded that area.

Like those in that region who were confronted by the man's demonic lunacy:

- I feel powerless when I watch families break up and there is nothing I can do.

- I sense the hopelessness that breaks the hearts of loved ones when they pray for some family member who seems so far from Jesus.

- I watch in despair as I see people make choices I know will lead them to ruin, but have no power to change the outcome.

- I wrestle with the helplessness I feel when disease attacks someone I love.

Make no mistake, those are marks of the kingdom of Satan—the tools of his trade. I see him at work and suffer anguish because it seems we are powerless to do anything about it.

The truth is, we are powerless, but He isn't! When Jesus shows up, He puts the Enemy to flight. When the awesome power of God shows up, Satan's power diminishes like a candle in a house fire.

Dutch Sheets, in his wonderful book *Intercessory Prayer,* relates a story of a hopeless and powerless man, enabled by the amazing power of God to deliver even the worst of demoniacs.

In 1976, during a missions trip to Guatemala to build tiny houses for a portion of the one million who were left homeless in an earthquake, they chanced upon a pitiful sight. Tied to a tree in the backyard of a small hut was a little girl. She was about 7 years old. She was filthy, helpless and alone. When they asked what was going on, they were told, "She is crazy. We can't control her. She hurts herself and others and runs away if we loose her. There is nothing else we can do for her, so we just have to tie her up."[5]

Sheets heard the Lord speak to him to pray for the little girl. He argued with God, finally obeying the unction of the Holy Spirit. Telling them what he was doing, he called on Jesus to show up in the habitation of demons. I'll let his own words describe what happened:

Then I prayed.

On a moonlit night, in a tiny, remote village of Guatemala with only a handful of people as my audience, my life changed forever.

Jesus came out of hiding. He became alive: relevant . . . sufficient . . . available! A "hidden" Jesus emerged from the cobwebs of theology. A yesterday Jesus became a today and forever Jesus. A Galilee Jesus became a Guatemala Jesus. . . .

Yes, He set the little girl free. Yes, the village turned to Jesus. Yes, Jesus prevailed through a sent one![6]

Jesus can move in spite of the powers of darkness that oppose you today. He is the victorious ruler! Paul made this very clear in Colossians 2:15: "And having disarmed the powers and authorities, he made a public spectacle of them, triumphing over them by the cross."

The image Paul uses is that of a conquered king being forcefully led in a parade by his victorious foe. He was a king who once commanded armies, but now he is vanquished and on display. Paul tells us that is what happened to Satan. Jesus, through His death on the cross and His subsequent resurrection, defeated Satan once and for all. Because of the Cross, because of the events of that bloody day outside Jerusalem, Jesus can move in demonic places—places of hopelessness and despair—and bring about life and renewal, giving hope and a future.

Do you remember the condition of that horrible man, David Berkowitz? If ever there were a hopeless situation, David was in the middle of it. Sentenced in 1978 to 365 consecutive years in prison, he was, in effect, buried behind bars. But that's not the end of the story. Ten years into his sentence, a man named Rick walked up to the notorious killer and told him about Jesus. One night, in desperation, the Son of Sam read Psalm 34:6: "This poor man called, and the Lord heard him; he saved him out of all his troubles."

Here are David's own words:

> It was at that moment, in 1987, that I began to pour my heart out to God. Everything seemed to hit me at once. The guilt from what I did . . . the disgust at what I had become . . . late that night in my cold cell, I got down on my knees and I began to cry out to Jesus Christ. I told Him I was sick and tired of doing evil. I asked Jesus to forgive me for all my sins. I spent a good while on my knees praying to Him. When I got up it felt as if a very heavy but invisible chain that had been around me for so many years was broken. A peace flooded over me. I did not understand what was happening. . . .
>
> I was involved in the occult and I got burned. I became a cruel killer and threw away my life as well as destroyed the lives of others. Now, I have discovered that Christ is my answer and my hope. He broke the chains of mental confusion and depression that had me bound. Today, I have placed my life in His hands. I only wish I knew Jesus before all these crimes happened. . . .[7]

Jesus showed up in a demonic man's prison cell and set him free. Because of the love and power of God, you and I one day will inherit heaven with a man who was formerly a demon-possessed convicted murderer. If there is hope for David Berkowitz, there is hope for that situation confronting you.

No power Satan can muster is able to withstand the power of God that will flow through our lives if we will totally yield ourselves to the Holy Spirit. No demonic force can long hinder a church that makes the decision to come together in unified prayer and fasting. Regardless of the spiritual despondency that may saturate the atmosphere of the church you attend, even the most incorrigible of evil spirits will take flight when God shows up in power and glory. In their place will come the refreshment of revival and glorious freedom found in Jesus Christ.

<h1 style="text-align:center">9</h1>

God Will Move in Destroyed Places

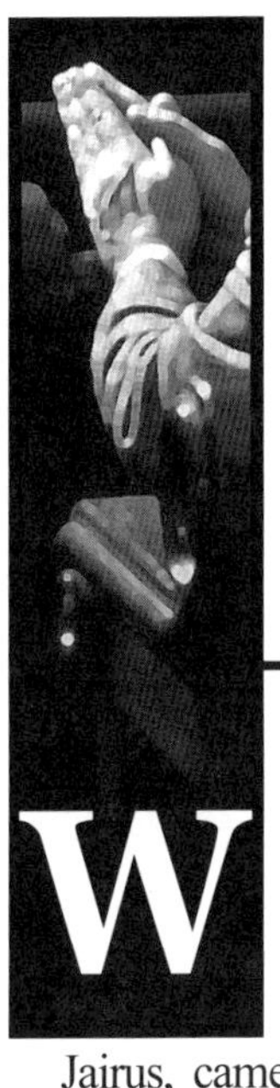

hen Jesus had again crossed over by boat to the other side of the lake, a large crowd gathered around him while he was by the lake. Then one of the synagogue rulers, named Jairus, came there. Seeing Jesus, he fell at his feet and pleaded earnestly with him, "My little daughter is dying. Please come and put your hands on her so that she will be healed and live." So Jesus went with him. A large crowd followed and pressed around him. And a woman was there who had been subject to bleeding for twelve years. She had suffered a great deal under the care of many doctors and had spent all she had, yet instead of getting better she grew worse. When she heard about Jesus, she came up behind him in the crowd and touched his cloak, because she thought, "If I just touch his clothes, I will be healed." Immediately her bleeding stopped and she felt in her body that she was freed from her suffering. At once Jesus realized that power had gone out from him. He turned around in the crowd and asked, "Who touched my clothes?" "You see the people crowding against you," his disciples answered, "and yet you can ask, 'Who touched me?' "But Jesus kept looking around to see who had done it. Then the woman, knowing what had happened to her, came and fell at his feet and, trembling with fear, told him the whole truth. He said to her, "Daughter, your faith has healed you. Go in peace and be freed from your suffering." While Jesus was still speaking, some men came from the house of Jairus, the synagogue ruler. "Your daughter is dead," they said. "Why bother the teacher any more?" Ignoring what they said, Jesus told the synagogue ruler, "Don't be afraid; just believe." He did not let anyone follow him except Peter, James and John the brother of James. When they came to the home of the synagogue ruler, Jesus saw a commotion, with people crying and wailing loudly. He went in and said to them, "Why all this commotion and wailing? The child is not dead but asleep." But they laughed at him. After he put them all out, he took the child's father and mother and the disciples who were with him, and went in where the child was. He took her by the hand and said to her, "Talitha koum!" (which means, "Little girl, I say to you, get up!"). Immediately the girl stood up and walked around (she was twelve years old). At this they were completely astonished. He gave strict orders not to let anyone know about this, and told them to give her something to eat (Mark 5:21-43).

The fifth chapter of Mark is considered by many to be the home of the incurable. In this chapter we meet three individuals who have been destroyed by powers opposing them. We have already looked at the demoniac, seeing that Jesus can indeed move in demonic places. Many consider this amazing deliverance impossible, but the cases of restored lives in verses 21-43 loom even larger.

We see the pernicious work of Satan in the accounts of the demoniac, the woman with the issue of blood and Jairus' daughter. Each person is hopeless, facing nothing but certain destruction and loneliness. If we met this trio today, we would call the police to have the man committed, and the health department and an ambulance to take the woman to an institution that cared for the terminally ill. As for the little girl—there would be no hope for her. We would help the brokenhearted father look for insurance papers and start cooking a post-funeral meal.

We would do all that because we are absolutely powerless against the destructive power of Satan, sin, sickness and death. But, we often forget, in our times of desperation, that Jesus is not powerless. These poor souls were beyond help. All possibilities and remedies had been expended. But Jesus was passing by and that would change things.

Today if we could only touch Jesus as He passes, we would never be the same. Demons couldn't stop us. Sickness couldn't confine us. Even death would not scare us because Jesus moved in our lives.

Here's the wonderful news . . . *He is here!* In this room where I sit writing. There where you are, Jesus says, "For where two or three come together in my name, there am I with them" (Matthew 18:20).

His promise will never fail—He is present in church every time we show up. Our problem is perception. We have grown so accustomed to an "experience" at church, so acclimated to the presence of the Holy Spirit, that we tend to take Jesus for granted. We overlook the fact that every time we gather in His name, His awesome presence is with us. His ability to reach into the scorched earth of destruction and transform it into a flourishing garden of beauty is overlooked. All that is required of us is to reach out and touch Him as He moves in our midst.

A Singing Parade

"When Jesus had again crossed over by boat to the other side of the lake, a large crowd gathered around him while he was by the lake" (Mark 5:21). Can you imagine that crowd? Think about who must have been in that group. I imagine that the former demoniac was there, along with the people Jesus had healed of leprosy and fevers.

Matthew 8 contains accounts of Jesus' healing many people and setting others free from demon-possession. I imagine a number of them were present that day. Maybe the centurion, or someone from his household, was present with Jesus that day. I think it was a singing crowd, excited because Jesus had done powerful things for them.

I am amazed at how silent we get when it comes to Jesus, because most of us have seen Him do some rather amazing things in our lives. Some of us would be dead today had it not been for the intervention of Jesus. Others would still be struggling in sin, fighting to get ahead, trying to cast off dubious habits, had it not been for the intervention of Jesus. Every one of us would be destined for an eternal hell—indeed, some would be there already, had it not been for the merciful intervention of Jesus. How can we possibly be silent when He has been so evident in our lives?

One day Jesus was entering a city. People were singing, shouting, much like this crowd. Some of the religious group was offended by the open praise. This group is always offended by open praise. But Jesus had an answer ready: "I tell you . . . if they keep quiet, the stones will cry out" (Luke 19:40).

Jesus was saying that He was so deserving of praise and singing that, if the people refused to respond, inanimate objects like stones on the side of the road would be divinely energized to worship. What an exciting moment that must have been.

Wouldn't it be terrible if, because we fail to worship, He had to energize someone or something else? Wouldn't it be tragic for the Lord, who has done so much for us, to find us unwilling to worship Him? How do you think it must feel for the Lord to deserve praise from us, His bride, and instead He has to go out and energize some drunk sinner to give Him praise? Wouldn't it be tragic if Jesus wanted praise and singing from us today and we were so reluctant to offer it that He decided to just accept it from the birds and crickets?

I don't know about you, but I plan to be part of a singing parade! I plan to be part of a worshiping group who offers praise to the Lord.

If you could see where Jesus brought me from, compared to where I am right now, you might have some idea of why I want to worship the way I do. If you could see the guilt, the sin, the sickness, the inner turbulence from which He has set me free, you would better understand my intense desire to bless His holy name. I love what the psalmist said:

Blessed are the people who know the joyful sound! They walk, O Lord, in the light of Your countenance. In Your name they rejoice all day long, And in Your righteousness they are exalted (Psalm 89:15, 16, *NKJV*).

I love the joyful sound. I love to praise the Lord for His greatness and splendor. I, for one, am glad we have made a shift from the doleful laments that glorified our troubles and pessimism. I am thankful we have turned from the sad sentiments of yesteryear that always talked about how bad things were and have turned our eyes heavenward and started singing to the Lord about how wonderful He is. I love it when we come and, in one accord, lift up the name of Jesus. Apparently, so does the Lord. He shows up when we praise Him.

A Sad Party

It is a fact of life that some of us will be singing while others will be sad. We migrate from one group to another. Before long, a sad party confronts the singing parade.

First, a man of great importance and prestige shows up who has a daughter who is dying. Even though this ruler of the synagogue had status and clout, that did not matter at the moment. He had a little girl back home who was terribly ill. In all probability, she was already dead by the time Jairus reached Jesus. He implores the Lord to come and touch his little girl.

Then one of the synagogue rulers, named Jairus, came there. Seeing Jesus, he fell at his feet and pleaded earnestly with him, "My little daughter is dying. Please come and put your hands on her so that she will be healed and live." So Jesus went with him (Mark 5:22-24).

I find it interesting that this fellow would probably have looked at Jesus with disdain and disgust in other circumstances—people like him were the very ones who plotted and schemed to kill Jesus. But, when the need became pressing, he threw his pride and his religious convictions out the window, came and fell down in front of this "mad man" and begged Him to come heal his daughter. Mercifully, Jesus consented.

Along the way, right in the middle of the crowd, a little skeleton of a woman appeared. Climbing under, over, around, any way she had to go, she pressed past the people and into the immediate presence of the Lord. She had been sick for 12 years and was getting worse. Nothing helped her; she had tried it all. If you went to her house and opened her cabinets, you would find prescription bottles and potions. Her frail, emaciated body bore marks from the attempts of the doctors of the day to make her better.

There were three things she did not have: strength, because it had been destroyed; money, because her savings had been eaten up in an attempt to get better; and time, because she was getting progressively worse. It wouldn't be long until she could no longer move about and she would die a terrible and lonely death.

We are told she had a *plague* (KJV), rendered *suffering* in the *New International Version*. The basic meaning of the word used here is "whip." Her plague had been used like a whip to beat her down and drive her away from the things she loved. Like a whip, it cut her out of the crowd and caused her to drop out of church. Like a whip, it singled her out and ostracized her from friends and loved ones. Perhaps worst of all, this poor lady, almost gone, had no one to run interference for her and get her to Jesus.

It makes me wonder how many people come to church, week after week, and feel isolated and alone. How many feel there is no one to advocate for them and get them to someone who can help? Is it possible that people flock to our churches Sunday after Sunday, hoping against hope that someone will introduce them to a life-giving, overcoming, powerful Jesus?

This woman had absolutely nothing left to give. For her, it was just about over. But somehow she managed to touch the outer edge of the tunic of the Lord. There was no anointing oil on her head, no shouting evangelist, no gimmicks or money raising. She was just a desperate woman touching the fringe of a garment worn by Jesus. But friend, that's all it takes.

Something flowed out of Jesus and He knew it. He stopped right in His tracks and demanded to know who touched Him. Dim-witted and closed-minded, the disciples saw only the physical. There were hundreds, probably thousands, of people jostling around Jesus. He wanted to know who touched Him. He stopped and demanded to know. Jesus did not want to know so He could reprimand her, but so that He could complete the wondrous work begun in the woman.

Remember, He was on the way home with a synagogue ruler to heal his daughter. Every moment was crucial. And now, here He was, stopping! I can imagine Jairus thinking, *We need to get this show on the road.*

But Jesus, in His compassionate way, demonstrated something everyone of us needs to grasp—Jesus is never too busy for *you*! He will stop in the middle of all the chaos of the times and touch you. Jesus is not too busy taking care of the "big boys" to stop what He is doing and touch the lowest of the low.

Compare Jairus and the sick woman and tell me who would get attention from some of the so-called servants of Jesus today:

- We know the name of Jairus from history; we have no idea of the identity of the woman.

- Jairus was a powerful political figure; the woman had no clout.

- Jairus had powerful and influential friends; the woman was alone in the world.

- Jairus had money and rich friends; the woman was dead broke.

- Jairus was freshly scrubbed and attired in the finest of suits; the woman wore smelly, dirty rags.

As much as I hate to admit it, in most churches, in most crusades, Jairus would be sitting on the platform and the woman would be up in the balcony, if she could even get in. Men would clamor to Jairus, but they would tend to ignore the woman. But Jesus isn't like the rest of us! He will stop at a moment's notice what He is doing with the most prominent evangelist on earth to touch a grandmother who has no money. He will reach right past the most influential person in the church to lift up and energize a stranger.

While Jesus is healing the woman, the well-known and powerful Jairus is pacing. Suddenly, he hears the news he dreaded most—his daughter was dead. The messenger tells him, "Your little girl is dead. Don't bother the teacher any longer."

That messenger was wrong on two counts. First, it never bothers Jesus to hear our cry. We are not harassing the Lord when we cry out to Him. He never tires of hearing us call on His name. Quite the contrary, He relishes the opportunity to have us call on His name. Over and over again we are entreated to cry out to the Lord. From what I understand about the teaching of Jesus, we should cry out and call on His name until we have the answer.

> "Ask and it will be given to you; seek and you will find; knock and the door will be opened to you. For everyone who asks receives; he who seeks finds; and to him who knocks, the door will be opened" (Matthew 7:7, 8).

Those verbs are in the present tense. That means we are to ask, and keep on asking; knock, and keep on knocking; seek, and keep on seeking. We never wear out the Lord. He wants us to call on His name.

The second mistake made by the messenger was what he called the Lord. He called Him "teacher." Understand, Jesus is a teacher—He is the Master Teacher. But, if all He happens to be is a teacher, we are in trouble. A teacher cannot do one thing about a demonic man, a decimated woman or a dead child. But, the Son of God can change things in an instant.

Jesus is more than a teacher. He is almighty. He is capable. He is able today to do more than any of us ask, think or imagine.

He can, in a moment of time, change a sad party into a singing parade. He can, in one moment of time, change your life from one of defeat and despair to one of victory and overcoming. He can move into a destroyed place and make it a delightful place. He can move into your church this Sunday and your place of worship will never be the same.

Supernatural Power

Jesus can do that because He has all the power that will ever be needed. Listen to His own words: "All authority in heaven and on earth has been given to me" (Matthew 28:18).

The word *authority* means capacity, force, privilege or mastery. The resurrected Jesus has no money, no army, no organization; but the one thing He does possess is the means to change the world. He has the supernatural power needed to change lives. Just as He changed the lives of that bunch that day, He can change us today.

Here were two groups: one happy, one sad; one singing, one sighing. Jesus came along and made them one. Those who were crying left rejoicing. A woman who was dying left healed. A brokenhearted family suddenly had new life given.

All this took place because God moved into some destroyed places and brought new life. He hasn't changed since then. Anything He did then, He can do today.

Still not convinced that God can do anything about your situation? Don't take my word for it. Find someone who has experienced what I am talking about. They are in church with you all the time. They will tell you how they entered the presence of the Lord sighing, but left singing. They can testify to the ability of Jesus to take the wrecked, ruined, even destroyed places in their lives and breathe life into them. They can tell you firsthand about the power of our Lord to break the grip of hopelessness. They are all around us because of the ability of God to show up in wreckage and bring life.

section three

God's Promises

10

I Will Build My Church

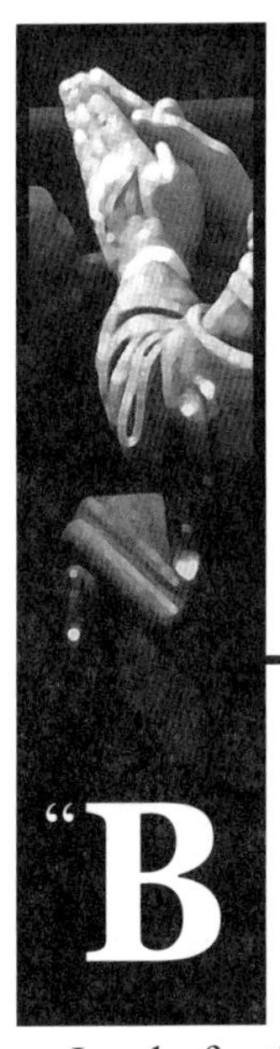

"But what about you?" he asked. "Who do you say I am?" Simon Peter answered, "You are the Christ, the Son of the living God." Jesus replied, "Blessed are you, Simon son of Jonah, for this was not revealed to you by man, but by my Father in heaven. And I tell you that you are Peter, and on this rock I will build my church, and the gates of Hades will not overcome it. I will give you the keys of the kingdom of heaven; whatever you bind on earth will be bound in heaven, and whatever you loose on earth will be loosed in heaven" (Matthew 16:15-19).

We have considered our desperate need for a move of God and we realize that without His help, we cannot survive, much less build His church. As bleak as that assessment may sound, it is true. The world is fed up with our superficiality and hypocrisy. They see through us like a thin piece of tissue paper. The church is amazingly gullible. When it comes to the fraudulent practices of the flashy and glitzy, the church has little, if any, discernment left. If it looks good, sounds good, and appeals to certain natural senses within us, it must be God.

The world is turned off to that junk and won't show up. We make the mistake of interpreting their absence at our festivals as a sign that the church is finished. Gloomy pundits have written the obituary of the church for decades, calling for her funeral and burial. All the while, God has continued to build His church.

That's His promise—He will build His church! We can be part of it, if we want to. The key to survival is the understanding that God is building His church. His church may look nothing at all like we think it should, but He has been, is, and will be, building His church.

The writer of Hebrews makes an astounding statement: "Therefore, since we are receiving a kingdom that cannot be shaken, let us be thankful, and so worship God acceptably with reverence and awe, for our 'God is a consuming fire'" (12:28, 29).

The word *shaken* has the meaning of being toppled, destroyed, rocked, disturbed or incited. The Word of God is telling us that none of the mocking criticism the world hurls at the church hinders God one bit. All the threats, all the fist-shaking, all the ranting and raving through the centuries against the church and her Christ haven't raised God's blood pressure one point. Men can scream and do their worst, but God just keeps on building His church.

After all, that's what He promised He would do. You can count on this one thing: *There will be a church!* God will make sure of that.

The church that God will build, protect and nurture may not look anything at all like our conception of what the church should be. Remember, God said He was going to build *His* church, not ours.

Think of the modern, especially American, image of what a real church is.

- It is large, or on the way to becoming large in a hurry.

- It has the latest technological gadgets.

- Everything is done in a showy and flashy manner.

- Preaching is timed to the exact minute.

- Nothing offensive is ever said or done.

- You are in and out in an hour.

- Everyone, from the infants to the oldest seniors, has a specialized ministry.

There is nothing wrong with those things. What's wrong is when we start to think God has to have all those things to build His church. As painful as it is for us to admit, not one of those things was in vogue when the events recorded in the Book of Acts took place, and God still managed to build His church in the midst of the worst persecution imaginable.

God does not need our flashy talents. He needs our available weaknesses. He is not short on gifted persons. He uses broken vessels that will depend upon Him for power and anointing. The pressing need in God's church has never been people with great gifts. He needs broken, spilled-out individuals who will bow at His feet and allow Him to flow through them with power and grace.

A recent article in *Current Thoughts and Trends* describes the ability of God to build His church. Taken from "Success Under the Cross," by Johnathan Chao in *Modern Reformation*, the story relates the power of God to build His church in China.

> In 1950 there were approximately 850,000 Protestant Christians in communist China. Today there are an estimated 85 million. The Chinese church's model of growth may be "successful," but it comes at a price most Westerners would be loath to pay . . . persecution.[1]

The article lists reasons why the church is flourishing and the ways in which God builds His church. In our day of "easy-believism" and "seeker-sensitive" church services, you probably won't hear a great deal about these methods. However, they are the tried-and-true systems that God has used since the inception of the church. If they have worked for centuries, and are working today, it might do us well to look once again at the patterns God uses. It's time we listen to those who are experiencing a move of God like those recorded in the Book of Acts.

Several years back, at a General Assembly (an international conference held in my denomination), I heard the great preacher Charles Blake speak on this issue. He told us, "If the bait you are using isn't catching any fish, why not switch over to the bait that is loading the boat?" God is building His church. He might not be building my church or your church, but He is building His church. The time has come for us to stop making excuses about our diminishing churches and start using some of the same bait those building the Kingdom with great success are using. It is time we hand over the keys, surrender our position of power and say, "God, from this moment forward, this is *Your* church. Do with it as You please!"

When we say that, and really mean it, God will honor our commitment. But the devil is lurking around every corner, listening to the prayers of commitment we pray. Rest assured, he will challenge us when we dedicate ourselves to the Lord.

Through Tough Times

In China, the church is growing in the midst of intense persecution. "Those undergoing persecution report that it has deepened their spiritual life and caused them to scrutinize their lives and ministries."[2] What a profound statement. Tough times have made them disciplined believers who can evaluate what is really necessary in church. Amazingly, the thing they seem to find necessary happens to be church itself:

Think about what's most important to us in church today.

- Some tell us it is the ladies restroom and nursery facilities.

- Others think it is comfortable surroundings.

- Some people base their decision about a church on sound, programs, preaching style, or a thousand other selling points.

- Many want up-to-date electronics and glitzy shows.

- Some base their choice on how friendly a church is or what options are offered.

- Heaven forbid we have trouble getting our favorite parking space or seat!

In other words, we make our choices based on what appeals to us. If something strikes us wrong, we are out of there in a flash, searching for whatever scratches our itch. If it isn't easy, we drop out.

In this case, we perceive the church as our possession, and God never made one commitment to preserve anything belonging to us. God is building *His* church around the globe today. *His* church is sold out. *His* church doesn't care what the surrounding circumstances are like. *His* church is on fire and growing like never before. *His* church is interested in one thing, and one thing only: to serve and please Jesus Christ. Nothing else matters. *His* church wants *Him*.

Is it possible that we, in our fervor to be accepted by the world, have sacrificed too many of God's precious gifts upon the altar of opinion? Think about it for a moment. Have we, in our efforts to become big and important, started building our own kingdom and ceased to be His church? There is nothing wrong with being large in number or well spoken of in the community, as long as we do not neglect the Holy Spirit.

In my lifetime within the Pentecostal and Charismatic world, I have seen some mighty transformations. Years ago, we occupied the church across the tracks, if we were lucky. Those who claimed charismatic gifts were branded "heretics," "lunatics," "snake-handling fanatics," and other epithets. We appeared to take pride in being labeled misfits. We had a motto: "If you can name it, we will claim it!"

This is no longer the case. From the United States Senate, down through corporate America and into the legal and business establishments of our land, there are many who openly claim the charismatic gifts. On top of that, our buildings are far from the country churches that once dotted the landscape. Today, some local congregations boast state-of-the-art facilities with price tags in excess of $100 million.

With all this at our disposal, why are we not winning the United States to God? Could it be we have grown so "big" in our own eyes we are no longer available to the Lord? Saul, Israel's first king, is proof that this can happen.

> Samuel said, "Although you were once small in your own eyes, did you not become the head of the tribes of Israel? The Lord anointed you king over Israel. And he sent you on a mission, saying, 'Go and completely destroy those wicked people, the Amalekites; make war on them until you have wiped them out.' Why did you not obey the Lord? Why did you pounce on the plunder and do evil in the eyes of the Lord?" (1 Samuel 15:17-19).

When he was small, still depending on God for anointing and direction, Saul was a success. When he decided he was too big for even God to direct, things began to spin out of control and he wound up losing everything.

Once again, we need to get our focus off good times, financial affluence and recognition by men. We must remember this: Without Him, we can do absolutely nothing!

Having a tough time? Don't sweat it! God knows how to take tough times and bring a great harvest into your life and into the church. He can take the hardest, bleakest, most desperate times and bring glory to His name in ways we have never dreamed possible. Let Him build you in your lean days and He will use you to bring forth a great harvest for His glory.

One Person at a Time

In China, to avoid persecution, house churches must remain small, but that doesn't slow growth at all. The larger groups just split up and form new groups. It isn't long until the new groups grow and, to avoid detection and persecution, they split again. That's foreign to our way of thinking. In a free society, the church doesn't have to function precisely that way, but the method in China does bring one truth home in a profound way: God saves us and builds His church one person at a time!

It's easy to get lost in a large church, but God knows you. He is interested in you. When we have pain and difficulty in our lives, we tend to see a crowd, but Jesus sees one . . . you!

All through His ministry, Jesus demonstrated this individual care.

- He stopped a procession to minister healing to one forgotten little lady.

- He stopped by a sycamore tree to reach out to one lonely tax collector.

- He ventured far out of His way to go to Samaria so He could meet with one sinful woman.

- He traveled across the sea to deliver one demon-possessed man.

- He took time out of a crowded situation to restore the sight of one blind man.

- Jesus will build His church one person at a time by taking time to minister to you and your need.

Regardless of how out of the loop you think you are right now or how unloved or lonely you feel, God cares for you as a person, as an individual. Your status or importance in the eyes of the world doesn't matter. Jesus will take the time to pause and reach out to you.

To Jesus, the outcasts of society matter a great deal. AIDS, cancer, ill repute—none of these things prevent Jesus from stopping to touch you.

> When he came down from the mountainside, large crowds followed him. A man with leprosy came and knelt before him and said, "Lord, if you are willing, you can make me clean." Jesus reached out his hand and touched the man. "I am willing," he said. "Be clean!" Immediately he was cured of his leprosy (Matthew 8:1-3).

We fail to understand how dramatic this one act was. Jesus reached out and touched the man." It was forbidden, socially unthinkable to touch a leper. You passed them by, keeping your distance.

Not Jesus! He was busy touching the world, building His church one at a time. If a leper wanted to be part, so be it. The same should be true today. If a social outcast wants to be part of His church, welcome. If the dregs of society want to become part of His family, welcome. If the lonely and isolated and those who feel no one cares want to be part of His church, welcome. One by one, He will heal, forgive, cleanse and welcome anyone to become part of His family.

The powerless in society matter. Those who are poor and exploited by the world's political machinery matter to Jesus. He will stop the fast-paced world around us to touch anyone who will dare to call on His name.

Then little children were brought to Jesus for him to place his hands on them and pray for them. But the disciples rebuked those who brought them. Jesus said, "Let the little children come to me, and do not hinder them, for the kingdom of heaven belongs to such as these." When he had placed his hands on them, he went on from there (Matthew 19:13-15).

The reader can almost see hordes of little kids clamoring all around the place, while parents hover around Jesus like modern-day autograph seekers, crying out for Him to touch their little ones. And the disciples? Like most of us, they had more urgent business to tend to than the children.

But Jesus stopped what He was doing and adjusted the attitudes of His disciples right on the spot. Why? Because the weak and powerless have a special place in the kingdom of God. They occupy a soft spot in His great heart and He has made a commitment to minister to them. So, if you have no power, no politician pulling for you, no inside track in the company, no rich uncle leaving you his wealth—if you are one of the vast sea of commoners who feels powerless and overlooked—Jesus will not hesitate to lay His hand on your life today!

The hopeless of society do matter. They are all around us—the homeless, the drug addicts, the alcoholics who live under the bridges—the marginal edge of society. They are the group we feel a little uncomfortable around—that group of people who would cause a large number of church folk to look for another place of worship if they suddenly started filling the pews.

But Jesus is building His church with just such material. Look around. God is saving men who ran pornography businesses. God is building His church with former drug dealers. God is humbling mighty men who once occupied lofty places in government and building His church with them. Jesus is reaching into bars and night clubs and rescuing men and women, making them pillars in His church. Jesus is taking the "walking wounded" of our society and making them soldiers of the Cross.

One at a time, Jesus is doing today the exact thing He did with the woman suffering from the flow of blood. She had been cast out, marginalized by society—she had no hope and no one cared. But Jesus stopped a procession being led by a rich nobleman to heal her. He does the same today.

There is no question that God is exponentially building His church. People are being swept into the Kingdom in staggering numbers. But sinners always come in one at a time. Jesus hears each cry, no matter how small or feeble. He will hear yours right now if you will dare to speak His name.

God's Praying People

It comes as no surprise to find that the church in China is a group of praying saints. Anywhere God is truly building His church, you will find praying people. The method God is using in China is no different from the one He used in the early church. Chao notes, "Persistent persecution has turned the Chinese church into a prayer force. Indeed, because it has few resources besides prayer, the church's discipline in this area has resulted in tremendous advances."[3]

They are a prayer force. What a concept! Pray and believe God to move. That's how God builds His church. Of course, we have a different approach today; for instance, when we face a legal situation in the church, whether it is a rezoning proposal or the church's desire to build a building without the government's consent, what do we do? We hire the best lawyer money can buy and file a lawsuit. Then we contact every politician we know and threaten them with a loss of the church's vote next time around. If that doesn't work, we will appeal to the media to garner sympathy in the community.

That sounds good, and quite often it works. However, what if no lawyer would take the case because the church had no legal standing in the court system? What if you challenged a zoning law and wound up getting arrested for being a Christian and got executed for your trouble? What if we signed a petition and sent it to our local government representative and the next Sunday, a group of armed policemen stormed the church, beat up a few members, slapped a few women around and shot the pastor right in front of the whole congregation, all with the blessing of the politician? What if, instead of sympathetic support from the local media, you are publicly ridiculed and persecuted for being a Christian? Church attendance would decrease, I assure you.

That's precisely what the church faces in many parts of the world today. The church in China that is growing by leaps and bounds is a church of prayer because that's the only resource they have. That's the only resource they need.

When the heat was turned up and things started looking bad for the New Testament church, when they had no recourse, no political clout, no legal standing, no way to persuade the opposition confronting them, they did something most of us would find silly and futile: They prayed!

On their release, Peter and John went back to their own people and reported all that the chief priests and elders had said to them. When they heard this, they raised their voices together in prayer to God. "Sovereign Lord," they said, "you made the heaven and the earth and the sea, and everything in them. You spoke by the Holy Spirit through the mouth of your servant, our father David: 'Why do the nations rage and the peoples plot in vain? The kings of the earth take their stand and the rulers gather together against the Lord and against his Anointed One.' Indeed Herod and Pontius Pilate met together with the Gentiles and the people of Israel in this city to conspire against your holy servant Jesus, whom you anointed. They did what your power and will had decided beforehand should happen. Now, Lord, consider their threats and enable your servants to speak your word with great boldness. Stretch out your hand to heal and perform miraculous signs and wonders through the name of your holy servant Jesus." After they prayed, the place where they were meeting was shaken. And they were all filled with the Holy Spirit and spoke the word of God boldly (Acts 4:23-31).

Something in this passage catches my attention: rather than bumping off the bad guys, God simply built His church. He gave strength to His people. He empowered His church through prayer to face the enemy and overcome his tactics. That is precisely what God wants to do with His church today.

As much as it bothers us to come to grips with this truth, we must. God isn't going to remove all the enemies of the church! There will always be a Goliath on the scene, bellowing at God's people. Cut him down like David did and a brother will pop up somewhere. Get rid of them and some children or nephews will surface and carry on the family tradition of opposition to God's purpose. No, God isn't going to wipe them out. Instead, He is going to use them to get us to pray and get full of the Holy Spirit so we can be His instruments in this evil age.

Nothing is more important than this—if we fail in the closet of prayer, we will fail completely. Without prayer, we are not going to become part of the church God is building in the midst of the enemy's camp, and we will not have the resources necessary to be victorious in the battles ahead. Individually, we will not be able to sustain a walk with God. Collectively, we will not scratch the surface of effectiveness in the Kingdom.

But, if we will pray until the power of God shakes the very foundations of our lives, we will have what it takes to go out into a hostile world, assured of victory. When it is all said and done, God's church will stand.

Rome in all her glory is gone. Shattered ruins dot the landscapes of Europe and Asia, telling us she once extended there. Rome fell, but the church of Jesus Christ still stands! That's because the church learned how to pray when times got hard and brought the power of the Almighty to bear against the unassailable power of the enemy. Rome fell . . . Jesus still reigns! Calling on His name still works.

Flowing in His Spirit

Once again, considering what is happening in China, we can learn a powerful principle that is often overlooked. In our effort to be in control, we must realize that if we are God's church, He is going to lead us where He wants us to go, regardless of my opinion or the opinion of anyone else. That's hard to accept, especially for those who are in control and enjoy the feeling of power.

In China, things are slightly different. "As waves of persecution come, top house-church leaders are usually the first to be arrested . . . Persecution also forces the church to develop a fluid, yet tight, organizational structure and communication network, much like that of an army on the move."[4]

In other words, they are flexible to the leadership of the Holy Spirit. Sometimes, this arises out of necessity. They are not stuck in the mud with organizational control and bound by a "hold the fort until Jesus comes" mentality. They are an army on the move, ready to battle at any time.

What an idea! Hear from God, then go do what He says! Of course, it's easy to be flexible when you have a new pastor every few months because the last one is now in prison for preaching the gospel. It's easier to be flexible when you meet in someone's house for church for a few weeks and then are assigned to a new house because the one you have been attending has outgrown the facility or has been shut down by the government.

But, is it at all possible that we have entrenched ourselves in His church so much that we have forced Him out? Could it be possible that Jesus wants to move in His church but our intractable attitudes won't allow Him access?

Jesus describes the ways of the Holy Spirit in this scripture: "The wind blows wherever it pleases. You hear its sound, but you cannot tell where it comes from or where it is going. So it is with everyone born of the Spirit" (John 3:8).

He is telling us the Holy Spirit moves at will. Jesus compares the moving of the Holy Ghost to the blowing of the wind. When the wind blows, you might be able to tell its direction. The path of a tornado is very traceable, but that's about the limit of our knowledge.

The Holy Spirit is a dynamic, living presence in His church. He refuses to be a boxed commodity we dole out as we please. His desire, His unchangeable purpose, is to flow through His church with His Spirit as He pleases. That upsets some of us and causes us to revolt. It is, nevertheless, the truth of God's Word.

Dr. Jack Deere authored one of my favorite books, *Surprised by the Power of the Holy Spirit.* In it, he chronicles his journey from a stuffy professor of theology who was convinced the working of the Holy Spirit was relegated to occasional occurrences, to a full-fledged believer in the power of the Holy Spirit to move mightily in the earth today. By his own account, he was a structured, rigid, tightly defined theologian who was convinced he had all the answers. He had a system of beliefs and balances that added up to a God who was predictable, patterned and, to be honest, powerless. Within his framework, God could slip in every once in a while because He was, after all, God, but that was rare and questionable when it happened.

Then, everything changed when a speaker came to a conference at his church and the Lord showed up. His problem was with *how* the Lord showed up. It didn't fit his pattern. God delivered a woman from a troubling demonic oppression and it really bothered him. He was happy the lady was set free, but Deere faced the same dilemma we all face when this uncontrollable, consuming-fire, thunder-and-lightning God shows up—we must either go with the flow or build a dam.

He opened the Bible and read the story of the demoniac of Gadara. A more powerful story of the moving of the Holy Spirit in the life of Jesus is not recorded. His eyes fell on the very end of the story.

> Those who had seen it told the people how the demon-possessed man had been cured. Then all the people of the region of the Gerasenes asked Jesus to leave them, because they were overcome with fear. So he got into the boat and left (Luke 8:36, 37).

Here is what Deere says: "I was on the verge of doing just what the Gerasenes had done . . . In great mercy the Lord Jesus Christ had visited our church. He had sent the Holy Spirit to prompt confession and uncover hidden demonic power in order to strengthen and heal us. And now I was on the verge of asking Him to leave because I was afraid of how some people might respond."[5]

When God moves outside our tightly defined boundaries, we have to make a choice. Do we go with God and risk it all or retreat to the safety of our well-scripted rituals? The real question we should be asking is not "Is God going to move?" or "Can God move here or in my life?" God is moving today. The real question we need to ask ourselves in a very frank and honest time of introspection is, "Are we willing to flow with what God wants to do rather than depending on the patterns of the past?"

Bud Williams makes a sad, but fitting, judgment of many of us when describing the reactions he has encountered in his quest for a fresh touch of God:

> We found that we needed an entire filing cabinet for the letter "P" for Pharisee. Many Christians, even Spirit-filled ones, were unmoveable, like wax idols from previous days of glory. They rejected the fresh fire of revival and chose instead to remain frozen in another period of history . . . Pharisees in a lifeless wax museum.[6]

We can look longingly at the ways God moved in days gone by and miss the next great movement of the Lord like a $100 bill blown by a gale-force wind under the nose of a beggar. We see it fly by, wish we had it, know how much we need it, but before we do anything about it, it is gone.

The days of sitting around and waiting on some group of men to tell us how to do God's work, how to build God's church, are over. We used to followed a strictly prescribed pattern set forth by a small group of well-meaning individuals. We read their books, listened to their stories and marched out into a lost world. Our focus was narrow, our field of vision limited.

Now we understand clearly how God moves in China, where He had been cut out of society for decades. The Spirit of the Lord moves there without all the slick plans men contrive. And China is just one place where God is building His church without the man-made patterns we find necessary.

The method is not the question. The means by which it is happening is all that matters. Perhaps it is time we stopped worrying about implementing a method from Chicago or California. Perhaps if we stopped going crazy trying to adopt the latest fad from Texas or conform to the hottest method from Florida, we would realize once again that the means by which the Kingdom operates, the flow of the Holy Spirit through our lives, is all that matters. We too could move forward and become *His* church once again. When that happens, He will build a church that even Satan himself cannot overcome.

Will being flexible under the leadership of the Holy Spirit cost us? You bet. It costs some leaders in China their freedom. Indeed, it costs some of them their lives. It cost Jack Deere his standing at a noted and famous seminary, his circle of friends, his church—even his job. It will cost us as well, should we dare to dislodge the rocks damming up the flow of God's Spirit. But what we receive will more than compensate for any losses. The glory of God in a church will more than make up for any people who decide they don't want to be part of what God is doing. The sheer joy of His presence will more than compensate for any lost friendships. The cattle-on-a-thousand-hills God we serve is quite capable of making up any lost finance some disgruntled member uses as a rock to inhibit the flow of the Holy Spirit.

Let's risk it! Let's hear from God and become flexible enough to bend with the wind of the Holy Ghost. Let's embrace the promise of God that He will build His church. Only then can we become truly His.

11

I Will Pour Out My Spirit

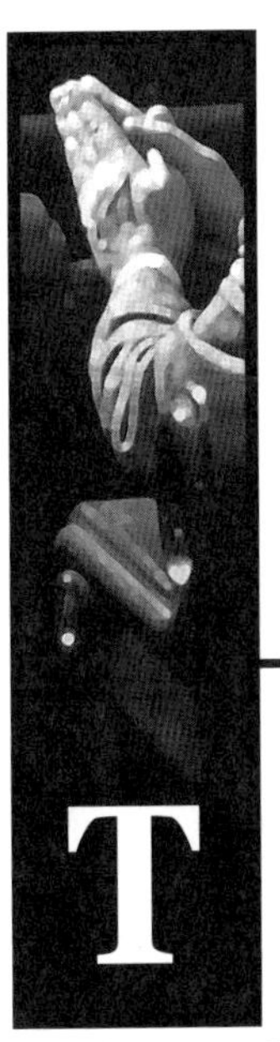

Then Peter stood up with the Eleven, raised his voice and addressed the crowd: "Fellow Jews and all of you who live in Jerusalem, let me explain this to you; listen carefully to what I say. These men are not drunk, as you suppose. It's only nine in the morning! No, this is what was spoken by the prophet Joel: 'In the last days, God says, I will pour out my Spirit on all people. Your sons and daughters will prophesy, your young men will see visions, your old men will dream dreams. Even on my servants, both men and women, I will pour out my Spirit in those days, and they will prophesy'" (Acts 2:14-18).

We are living in days of extremes. In the world of the church, things seem to have taken on a condition similar to what those in the psychiatric field call bi-polar disease. On the one hand, things are terrible. In the United States, we lose ministers every year by the thousands. We close thousands of churches that were once lighthouses of hope offered by Jesus Christ. Pressure is being applied to the church to back into a small, quiet corner and become less salt and light than in past days.

On the other hand, these are the best of times. As God promised, He is pouring out His Spirit all over the world. Great harvests of souls are being swept into the Kingdom in numbers which would stagger the minds of the apostles of the first century. Such numbers cause many to blink their eyes with astonishment.

- Africa was less than 5 percent Christian at the turn of the 20th century; it is estimated to be 50 percent Christian by now.

- China had only about 5 million believers when Communism took control of the country. Now the estimates vary from 50 to as high as 150 million believers. Missiologists estimate that between 25,000 and 35,000 are coming to Christ daily in China.

- Indonesia is the world's most populated Muslim nation, but the percentage of Christians has been progressing so rapidly that the government won't release accurate figures.[1]

When you take into account the powerful move of God in Latin America and in the Latin world overall, God is indeed pouring out His Spirit in a mighty way. People are getting saved like never before in history. There is even speculation that in some areas of the world, the birthrate into the kingdom of God is surpassing the natural birthrate. That's something to shout about!

God honors His Word. He will do what He said He would do. Our opinion of what He does, our judgment of what He is doing, even our willingness to participate in what He is doing, has absolutely no bearing on His promise. It is very clear that in the closing days of human history, He will make a worldwide sweep of His Spirit and all those who will accept what He is doing will be taken to a new spiritual level.

It all started on the Day of Pentecost, when the 120 staggered out of the Upper Room like drunk men. God began the final outpouring, and it continues today. Only now, it's not a gentle rain of glory or even the "tornado" that came into Jerusalem that day. No, today it is a category-five hurricane of God's Spirit ravaging the kingdom of Satan in ways I am sure our enemy never dreamed possible. It's a wave of the Spirit that renews moribund churches, dead and steeped with so much tradition the Holy Spirit is no longer welcome. Unshackled by the restraints of men long dead in the faith, the light of this experience goes out into a dark world and burns for Jesus with a passion many within the church once knew, but somehow lost along the way.

Can this new firebrand person make mistakes? Sure. Can he get off track? Of course. Can he be stopped? Well, as an individual, perhaps. But to try and stop what God is doing in these last days makes about as much sense as trying to fill up the Grand Canyon by throwing tiny marbles from Miami. You just aren't going to get the job done!

I think I am like many who have been serving Jesus for a long time. I am ready for an inundating downpour of the Spirit of God. I am weary of the balancing act of trying to please disgruntled sheep who will never be happy with any shepherd. I have grown despondent over our lack of ability to win people and make disciples. I grieve at the way our culture snubs and sneers at our powerless shows and ceremonies tainted with the glitz and glamor of the world. I am ready for a monsoon of His Spirit—a downpour—uncontrollable, unpredictable, unstoppable. I am ready to be a fresh part of the "all flesh" the Lord spoke of! Anybody want to take the trip with me?

Pouring Out His Spirit

For many in the Pentecostal and Charismatic circles, the ready answer to that question comes from Acts 2:

> When the day of Pentecost came, they were all together in one place. Suddenly a sound like the blowing of a violent wind came from heaven and filled the whole house where they were sitting. They saw what seemed to be tongues of fire that separated and came to rest on each of them. All of them were filled with the Holy Spirit and began to speak in other tongues as the Spirit enabled them (vv. 1-4).

Immediately we point to verse 4 and start to shout, "We speak in tongues! We speak in tongues!" While it is true that they did speak in other tongues, we need to face up to the fact that Acts doesn't end right there. There is more, so much more, to this outpouring than speaking in tongues. Sadly, many of us have experienced personal glossolalia and decided we have reached the pinnacle of spiritual effectiveness. In actuality, we have only begun the long journey into spiritual maturity.

When God pours out His Spirit, count on the fact that there will be fantastic signs such as speaking in tongues.

But there will be other things that will happen as well—things that will shake our lives even more than an ecstatic utterance given for personal edification.

When God pours out His Spirit, the hungry are fed—the needs of men are met by the power of God. To see this principle at work, simply observe the events that unfolded following the outpouring of the Spirit of God in the Upper Room on the Day of Pentecost. The pouring out of the Spirit of God met the needs of desperate humanity.

- Three thousand people, hungry for God, were saved.

- A man who had been unable to walk since birth ran around, shouting for joy.

- A church was shaken and revived, filled with boldness and a fresh touch of the Holy Ghost.

- Poor people had their needs met by those who were able.

- Multitudes were added to the church and spiritually hungry people were fed.

- Sick and demonically oppressed people were brought to Jerusalem and healed.

- Crowds of spiritually dead Samaritans found new life.

- An Ethiopian was saved and carried the gospel to Africa.

The list goes on and on. When God pours out His Spirit, people hungry for God will find Him. The question must be asked, "What are we hungry for?"

Are we hungry for a new life in Christ? We need an outpouring of God's Spirit. Are we hungry to be delivered from some habit or besetting sin? We need an outpouring of God's Spirit. Are we hungry to overcome, to rise above the circumstances that now confront us? We need an outpouring of God's Spirit. Are we hungry to see our families saved? We need an outpouring of God's Spirit. It sounds too simple to be true. Although there will be problems in the church regardless of how much God pours out His glory because we are flesh, until He pours out His glory once more, we are going to have a bunch of hungry people clamoring for bread we just can't produce. We need fresh fire—a new anointing.

Consider the Old Testament analogy of the power that accompanies the anointing of the Holy Spirit:

> Therefore thus says the Lord God of hosts: "O My people, who dwell in Zion, do not be afraid of the Assyrian. He shall strike you with a rod and lift up his staff against you, in the manner of Egypt. For yet a very little while and the indignation will cease, as will My anger in their destruction." And the Lord of hosts will stir up a scourge for him like the slaughter of Midian at the rock of Oreb; as His rod was on the sea, so will He lift it up in the manner of Egypt. It shall come to pass in that day that his burden will be taken away from your shoulder, and his yoke from your neck, and the yoke will be destroyed because of the anointing oil (Isaiah 10:24-27, *NKJV*).

The Lord says that the yoke will be broken because of the anointing of the Spirit. Now, take a close look at the rendering of the *New International Version*: "In that day their burden will be lifted from your shoulders, their yoke from your neck; the yoke will be broken because you have grown so fat" (v. 27).

God says through Isaiah, "I am going to give you so much anointing, you are going to swell. You are going to burst through the yokes that have held you back!" What a thought! God is going to pour out His holy anointing through His Spirit to the point that the yoke, the hindrance of Satan, will no longer work. It will be broken!

- The bondage of the past will no longer hold you captive.

- The old fears that once ruled you will no longer intimidate you.

- The chains that once held you down will no longer fit around your neck.

- Those things used by Satan to beat you down will no longer be effective.

When God pours out His Spirit upon us and we soak it up like a sponge, we are going to grow in His power and authority. The old things that used to cloak us and drag us down will no longer restrain us. Think of a man who has worked hard for many years in the gym and tries to put on a suit he wore in his early teens. Where there was no definition there are now ripples of muscle. What once fit will no longer suffice.

Similarly, when God pours out His Spirit in our lives, those old patterns Satan once used to defeat us will no longer be effective. We will have grown in power and will be able to stand our ground under the anointing. I'm ready to grow in God, how about you?

But there is more to God's outpouring than this. You see, when God pours out His Spirit, those who are hardened to Him get frustrated. Already set in their ways, crusted over with religion, the ones who do not wish to partake in a move of God's Spirit are always present and will always make their opinion known.

Our day is no different from the days of the early church. In the first century, there were plenty of antagonists around. And did they ever get frustrated! Again, the Book of Acts gives us a poignant snapshot:

> "But to stop this thing from spreading any further among the people, we must warn these men to speak no longer to anyone in this name." Then they called them in again and commanded them not to speak or teach at all in the name of Jesus. But Peter and John replied, "Judge for yourselves whether it is right in God's sight to obey you rather than God. For we cannot help speaking about what we have seen and heard." After further threats they let them go. They could not decide how to punish them, because all the people were praising God for what had happened. For the man who was miraculously healed was over forty years old (4:17-22).

I love the way *The Amplified Bible* states verse 17: "But in order that it may not spread further among the people and the nation, let us warn and forbid them with a stern threat to speak any more to anyone in this name [or about this Person]."

It doesn't take a rocket scientist to figure out what they meant by "a stern threat." Those boys wanted the apostles to lay off talking about Jesus or else!

In another location, we find them getting even more hostile and frustrated. It happened when Stephen, who was so anointed of the Holy Spirit that he witnessed Jesus at the right hand of the Father, told them the truth about the Lord. Note how these hardened men responded to a dose of truth:

> When they heard this, they were furious and gnashed their teeth at him. But Stephen, full of the Holy Spirit, looked up to heaven and saw the glory of God, and Jesus standing at the right hand of God. "Look," he said, "I see heaven open and the Son of Man standing at the right hand of God." At this they covered their ears and, yelling at the top of their voices, they all rushed at him, dragged him out of the city and began to stone him. Meanwhile, the witnesses laid their clothes at the feet of a young man named Saul (Acts 7:54-58).

That is *frustrated*! Grinding your teeth . . . shouting like a mad man . . . rushing a speaker like a bunch of crazed animals . . . running a guy out and stoning him to death. I would say the frustration meter was maxed out right about then.

So, we need to understand this: When God pours out His Spirit, some of the more religious among us are not going to like it one bit. What's more, they are going to let everybody who will listen know they don't like it.

In a church I pastored, a time of great revival came. Things started happening out of the blue. God showed up and made His presence known. People were saved. Some who had no intention of coming to church found themselves there that day and were saved. People were filled with the Spirit. Sick people were healed.

It was a tremendous time of outpouring. Guess what happened? Some of our best friends in the church decided they did not like this new freedom. They wanted the Holy Spirit, up to a point. But when things happened they didn't like, they bailed out. It felt like a punch in the solar plexus to me. But I learned this lesson: When God moves, hardened people—those unreceptive to anything but their own definition of a move of God—will get frustrated and try to hinder the move of God.

What do we do? We do the same thing they did in the first century. I like to call it a P&L statement. You might think that is looking at profit versus loss. Not really. I prefer to think of it as *praying* for those who won't go on with God and *looking* ahead to see what God wants to do in us. In other words, to foster a move of God, we have to develop the attitude of the old tune we used to sing: "If you don't go, it won't hinder me; I'm on my way, praise the Lord, I'm on my way!"

Besides the hungry getting fed and the hardened getting frustrated, another thing happens when God pours out His Spirit. This is the greatest thing of all—heaven gets filled! People get saved. Trace the outpouring of the Spirit through the New Testament or any great outpouring in history. Every time, without exception, you will find one common denominator—people were saved. Heaven was populated.

There have been many variations of manifestations—tongues, falling to the floor, visions and dreams, prophecies—but the one thing that was always present was salvation. The Kingdom was advanced because the Holy Spirit fell.

That leads me to this conclusion: If we are not winning people to Christ, if our altars are barren, if we are not seeing people brought to Jesus, we are not experiencing an outpouring of the Spirit of God regardless of how high we jump, how loud we shout, how worked up we become, or how emotionally satisfied we are when we leave church. God pours out His Spirit to save men and women. It's just that simple. If we really want to be part of the outpouring, we need to break out of our church services and spill over into our society and minister to those who are hungry for God and give them the fresh Bread of Life.

Why Not Here? Why Not Me?

With all God seems to be doing around the world, a very pointed question needs to be asked by every Christian in America, especially every Pentecostal and Charismatic Christian. It's a tough question few of us are ready to face, at least with honesty and integrity: Why not here? Why not me?

Before we start listing our top 10 reasons and making all our excuses, let's be honest and admit that most of us could stand to draw closer to God and have more of His Spirit at work in our lives. For all you supersaints (those who have it all together and have all of God's Spirit manifested in your life you will ever need), this might be a good time to check out. We'll pick you up next time when we talk about the coming of the Lord.

As a fellow traveler on the road to heaven and one who certainly could benefit from a greater move of God in my life, I have often asked this question: "What is the reason

God pours out His Spirit in one locale and not in another?" I have wondered many times, *Why does God move powerfully in a church in Iowa or Kansas, but not in a church in Alabama or Arizona? What makes the difference?*

I understand there are arguments about the sovereignty of God. Some are quick to claim that God is God, and He can do what He pleases. The Scriptures teach us that. However, a quick study of what the apostle Peter stated on the Day of Pentecost, coupled with a brief reading of the Scripture he quoted in Joel (2:28, 29), points out something very obvious—God is interested in pouring out His Spirit on everybody.

> "No, this is what was spoken by the prophet Joel: 'In the last days, God says, I will pour out my Spirit on all people. Your sons and daughters will prophesy, your young men will see visions, your old men will dream dreams. Even on my servants, both men and women, I will pour out my Spirit in those days, and they will prophesy'" (Acts 2:16-18)

The original prophecy, as well as the apostle's application, involves the wonderful promise of an across-the-board outpouring. That means this outpouring is for me, for my church, for my family, for my city. While God may decide to do a sovereign work in one particular locale or specifically gift one individual for a particular ministry, the outpouring of His Spirit is for everyone. That includes you and me!

What is our problem? Why are so many churches stagnant? Why have so many of us grown cold and indifferent? Why is it that the Holy Spirit appears to be red-hot in some corners of the globe while many of us sit in cold mausoleums called churches where no life has flickered in years? Why do I look in journals and magazines to read of individuals who are on fire for the Lord all around the world and find the embers of my own spiritual awakening dead and cold? Is it my fault? Is it society's fault? Is it God's fault?

The truth is hard to accept: the fault is my own. If I am dead to the move of God today, it's because I want to be. If my church is dead and no one is getting saved, it's because I want it that way. Hard words, for sure. But many of us need a wake-up call before it is too late.

I am sure there are many reasons why we are not experiencing a great outpouring of God's glory in our lives and churches, but three reasons are prominent every time we come together.

1. *We lack the willingness to completely surrender to Jesus.* In the preface to his book *Ten Lies About God,* Erwin Lutzer states, "We Americans, obsessed with consumerism and pleasure, have created a god who is tolerant of our lifestyles, lets us be in charge, and serves mainly to help us fulfill our potential. He is a god 'just for us.'"[2]

I hate to admit it, but he is right. The God preached today is very tolerant. He exists, so it seems, only to meet the desires of His people. He is a God who wants you to get your stuff and rise above your circumstances. I don't doubt one bit that Jesus wants us to possess the things He intends or that He wants to deliver us from a life crushed beneath the weight of our circumstances. However, that aspect of the Christian life seems to get major press, while the other, weightier messages of Jesus, get back-page billing—if they happen to be mentioned at all.

If you have a concept of Jesus as One who comes along only to bless you, make you feel better, and send you on your way into a blissful life of ease, you have contrived the wrong image. Jesus calls for—demands—absolute surrender. Our rebellion in this area is why we are not witnessing the spectacular outpouring of God's Spirit in our lives and churches.

Consider just a few commands—that's right, *commands*—from the lips of Jesus:

> "If anyone comes to me and does not hate his father and mother, his wife and children, his brothers and sisters—yes, even his own life—he cannot be my disciple. And anyone who does not carry his cross and follow me cannot be my disciple. . . . In the same way, any of you who does not give up everything he has cannot be my disciple" (Luke 14:26, 27, 33).

> Then Jesus said to his disciples, "If anyone would come after me, he must deny himself and take up his cross and follow me" (Matthew 16:24).

Add to this a quick study of what God said through Amos, the Old Testament prophet. His words have weighed heavily on me as I have pored over his prophecy. The scene is set—God is standing at the altar, pronouncing judgment on the people.

> I saw the Lord standing by the altar, and he said: "Strike the tops of the pillars so that the thresholds shake. Bring them down on the heads of all the people; those who are left I will kill with the sword. Not one will get away, none will escape. Though they dig down to the depths of the

grave, from there my hand will take them. Though they climb up to the heavens, from there I will bring them down. Though they hide themselves on the top of Carmel, there I will hunt them down and seize them. Though they hide from me at the bottom of the sea, there I will command the serpent to bite them. Though they are driven into exile by their enemies, there I will command the sword to slay them. I will fix my eyes upon them for evil and not for good" (Amos 9:1-4).

Isn't it interesting that judgment started at the altar? Right at the place where God's Spirit should be poured out upon the people, God brings judgment. The Lord tells them, "I am going to nail you to the wall! Nobody is going to escape!" He uses some vivid imagery. The grave is, of course, the place of the dead. Mount Carmel is a rugged and foreboding mountain. Both places speak of inaccessibility, but God can go where no man can venture. God says He is going to judge them regardless of how far they go or where they hide.

What on earth would cause the Lord to be so roused in anger against them? Had they turned from their religious practices and shut down the church? No. If you take the time to read the fifth chapter of Amos you will discover that they were still very religious. Of course, all their religious exercises did nothing to appease the anger of God. Conversely, all their religion added fuel to the fire of God's anger.

"I hate, I despise your religious feasts; I cannot stand your assemblies. Even though you bring me burnt offerings and grain offerings, I will not accept them. Though you bring choice fellowship offerings, I will have no regard for them. Away with the noise of your songs! I will not listen to the music of your harps" (Amos 5:21-23).

Pretty strong language, isn't it? They are doing all the religious stuff, but it is having zero effect on their lives. They are singing, dancing, bringing offerings, playing instruments, all in church and supposedly for the glory of God. But God can't stand it! Why? It's all an act! There's no surrender in their lives. They come and go through the motions of church, but they are acting just the same when they leave.

Here's a categorical list of things God said they were doing (vv. 7-12):

- Throwing down righteousness.

- Trampling the poor.

- Forcing the poor to give them grain.

- Building great mansions and lush vineyards while oppressing the poor.

- Taking bribes.

- Doing wrong in courts of justice—they had grown complacent and were pampering themselves with the very best of things while ignoring the plight of the poor.

Nobody was surrendering to the will or purpose of God. They were going to church, but there were no lasting effects. And God said, "I have had enough!" God wanted to do something *in* them more than He wanted to do something *for* them.

I face the same dilemma today. Either I surrender to God completely, do away with my false pretense of religion and become totally crushed in His presence, or persist in my own way until He comes to the altar of my heart in blistering judgment. That course of action is too terrible for me to contemplate.

Our churches face the same predicament. Will we totally yield to God or persist in having things our own way? One way displeases man but pleases God. The other makes men happy but leaves our Father standing outside knocking to get in.

I will say this: If we will surrender, die to self, abandon our own headstrong ways and submit to the program God calls for, He will do what He has promised. He will pour out His Spirit in our lives and bring about such an abundant harvest we will scarcely believe our eyes.

Consider the vivid image given by the Lord at the conclusion of Amos' prophecy:

"The days are coming," declares the Lord, "when the reaper will be overtaken by the plowman and the planter by the one treading grapes. New wine will drip from the mountains and flow from all the hills. I will bring back my exiled people Israel; they will rebuild the ruined cities and live in them. They will plant vineyards and drink their wine; they will make gardens and eat their fruit. I will plant Israel in their own land, never again to be uprooted from the land I have given them," says the Lord your God (9:13-15).

I hunger to see that day come to pass in my life and in my church. I long to see the time churches cannot build buildings fast enough to house the harvest the Lord sends in. I hunger to see the time churches are not haggling over transferring members, but reveling in the harvest of souls God is sending their way. I yearn for the day when the outpouring is so strong that those in bondage are set free and we rejoice together because of the liberty of the Lord.

But it will never happen to *my* church. It will never happen in *my* life. I will never see this in *my* denomination. Only when I lay at His feet and give up, die out, hand over the keys of *my* kingdom, will I witness the outpouring of His Spirit in my life. I'm ready to surrender. How about you?

2. *We won't worship.* Another major reason we are not experiencing an abundant anointing of the Spirit of God is the fact that we just won't worship God. Remember, worship brings His glory into our midst. I know . . . make a statement like that and you will have responses of fire heaped upon your head.

People will say things such as these:

- "I do worship!"

- "How dare you pass judgment on my worship!"

- "What I do in worship is between God and me; you stay out of it!"

I am passing judgment on no individual or church. That's not my place. God is the judge. However, I have looked around at the worship in places where God is pouring out His Spirit in great measures and in places where God isn't pouring out His Spirit in a great measure. The difference is in their worship. Where God is pouring out

His Spirit in great measure, people worship with excitement, with life, with abandon and no fear of what men have to say. They worship with exuberance, determination and fire. Those upon whom God is pouring out His Spirit have learned a simple lesson: Praise brings power.

On the other hand, lifeless religion, religion that changes no one, going-through-the-motions religion, is characterized by one common denominator: Worship has become a spectator sport, an entertainment exercise. This type of worship service begins and ends with—indeed, revolves around—*me*.

Instead of surrendering to God, I observe others who worship. I inspect, dissect, analyze, criticize, reflect and reject the attempts of others to worship. If I don't like it, I'll be sure to make it known. If it varies from my definition of what is good, I'll be sure to express my sentiments accordingly. If it upsets me, I'll certainly let the pastor know about it next week. Is it possible that our gradual shift from everyone worshiping to our modern entertainment craze within the church has so deadened us to real worship that many of us actually think we have worshiped God by coming to a weekend service, sitting on a pew, passing judgment on a choir, throwing a few dollars in a plate, and then giving a thumbs-up or thumbs-down on the whole show?

This is precisely what has happened and is one of the major reasons we sit spiritually idle in this land while God is moving in unprecedented ways all around us.

Honestly, what is real worship? I love what Richard Bieber says:

Worship: the human heart responding to glory that has come near, offering itself to God in thanksgiving, spending itself in praise. Worship cannot be engineered. No one can manipulate another person into a state of worship. Church leaders can turn down the lights, play soft music and invite us to close our eyes as we lift our hands. But it only becomes worship when we choose of our own free will to present our bodies to God as a living sacrifice, when we choose to lift our hearts to God in thanksgiving and praise.[3]

It is worship when you and I, of our own accord, fall to our knees or jump up and down. The posture is not the question. Until we give God the praise that He so richly deserves, He will not break the shackles of tradition and the pressures of our peers. We must simply abandon ourselves before the Father.

- Moses took off his shoes and came close to the bush, burning with God's glory.

- David threw off his kingship and became "common" before God and man in dance and song.

- In Nehemiah 9, the people stood for half a day in confession, repentance and worship.

- Isaiah, the great prophet, fell before the Almighty in confession, worship and submission.

- The lame man at the Temple gate, newly healed, leaped and ran all over the place.

- The crowd in the Upper Room, intoxicated with God's glory, spilled out into the city streets, shouting about the goodness of the Lord.

You and I must overcome our fleshly ideas and say, "I am going to worship God! I am going to overcome my fear of being made fun of and honor the Lord with all I have."

Spirit-filled churches across the land have well-trained choirs, great music programs and wonderful singers—but none of these constitute worship. Worship, and worship alone, brings His manifest presence into our lives. Worship is not the first part of the service. Worship *is* the service.

The psalmist made it clear: God dwells in worship. "But You are holy, enthroned in the praises of Israel" (Psalm 22:3, *NKJV*).

The word *enthroned* has many nuances. Among them are the following:

- His presence is manifested in our praises.

- His presence inhabits our praises.

- His presence is seated in our praises.

- His presence is settled in our praises.

It could even be said His presence is "married" in our praises. Married to what? To us!

How we need to worship, how we need to praise Him until He pours out His Spirit on our lives. Truthfully, we need this more than anything else on the planet.

Are you having trouble with the devil? There is a powerful way to confront and confound the forces of the Enemy that come against you. You can praise the Lord and watch the power of the Enemy be driven back!

Ron McIntosh relates the following incident from his life:

Recently, I had the privilege of seeing the deliverance and the restoration of a young woman who was an ex-Satanist.

We met together for several months in securing her freedom. During that time I would ask about the strategies of this demonic organization.

She told me that Halloween marks the beginning of the religious year for the satanic church. It is at this time that the leaders, among many other abominable practices, train followers to invade key churches in America. Their sole intent is to divide and destroy these churches.[4]

Her next bit of information is what really fascinated me since it concerns the principle of praise and worship.

"These infiltrators have the most difficulty weaving the destructive web in churches where they speak in tongues and where there is true worship," she said. "Why?" I asked. She responded, "Because praying in the Spirit, or true worship, throws the kingdom of darkness into confusion."[5]

One day, we are going to start praising the Lord in the midst of oppression, in the midst of trial, in the midst of persecution, in the midst of loss, and suddenly we are going to discover this dynamic truth: Praising God will bring the power of God! When that happens, His Spirit will begin to flow like never before in our lives. We *will* see the manifestation of the power of God for which we have longed!

3. *We have replaced working for Jesus with a meet-my-need mind-set.* We have, through a long process of seeking excellence in areas of ministry, transformed the church from an army of God to a bunch of spectators who assemble on a Sunday morning and watch while a "few good men" march around on God's parade ground. We

have totally reversed the order of things. We want the church to be a place where we sit by and watch God take a few people and make them sweat out there on the marching field. We want to argue about their uniforms. We like to debate about whether or not their styles are formal enough or too flamboyant. We want to note their cadence with a critical eye. We like to note how smoothly the service flows and how well we transition from commercial break back into the scheduled program. We certainly want to dissect the band playing for the marchers and the singers who are singing the anthem. After all, if they are off-key, something is wrong and needs to be addressed. The speaker had better not speak too long because these bleachers are, after all, hard and uncomfortable.

What an absurd joke. Nowhere in the Bible do you find one shred of evidence for the modern "take care of me and mine" mentality that cripples us today. You can find plenty of things to the contrary:

- "Endure hardship with us like a good soldier of Christ Jesus" (2 Timothy 2:3).

- "So do not be ashamed to testify about our Lord, or ashamed of me his prisoner. But join with me in suffering for the gospel, by the power of God" (2 Timothy 1:8).

- "Remember those earlier days after you had received the light, when you stood your ground in a great contest in the face of suffering" (Hebrews 10:32).

- "Blessed is the man who perseveres under trial, because when he has stood the test, he will receive the crown of life that God has promised to those who love him" (James 1:12).

Suffering? Persecution? Hardship? Trial? Prison? I'll pass on those, thank you. That is one reason we are soft. That's one of the reasons people get mad every time we turn around in church and storm off to the next place. And that's why we have become self-absorbed and so inwardly focused that nearly everything done in the church in America is done so we can keep the peace and maintain our current status.

On the surface, it appears that was beginning to happen in the early church. They fought the same things we fight today. They became a self-absorbed, "let them come to Jerusalem and get it" church.

By the time Acts 8 was written, they were comfortably settled in Jerusalem. They had made a few ventures outside the city, but by and large, they were still hanging around the Temple and staying Jewish in their outlook. It's easy to get self-absorbed and petty when you are just hanging around and getting blessed. They were having a fairly good time of things in the first few chapters of Acts. Even when a few preachers were beaten, somebody was healed and that made it worthwhile. By the end of Acts 4, everybody was having their needs met in a grand social experiment that ended later in disaster.

Guess what's next on the agenda for the church? Griping! That's right, griping and complaining. One group started complaining about how the other group was treated. Never mind that people were being saved and wonderful things were happening. The complaints started surfacing.

One day, someone who couldn't care less about the outpouring of the Holy Ghost whined, "I got two pieces of bread and she got three!" Can you believe that? I can, because I have been given the pleasure of standing as a referee in the middle of some things that were just about as important as that. The names changed, and so did the cause of the complaint, but the philosophy is exactly the same. Never mind that people need to be saved. Never mind the world is dying and going to hell all around us.

- I want my parking place.

- I want my job in church.

- I want my favorite song sung.

- I want my way on this committee.

- I want my vote to prevail.

- I want my traditional style.

- I want it my way, or else.

Heaven help us! We need to take a long, hard look at what happens next in Acts. Things heat up a bit when two good church members are killed by the Lord for lying. But what's a couple of people when we all have our needs met? Just be sure not to lie on your tithe form. Things proceed on fairly well from that point. The church grows . . . in Jerusalem.

But God did not want them to be a tiny, self-serving group. He intended for them to take the message of the Cross and deliverance to the ends of the earth. So, He rained on their parade in Jerusalem when the Lord allowed one of His own precious ones to be killed. Stephen, the first martyr of the faith, was stoned.

> And Saul was there, giving approval to his death. On that day a great persecution broke out against the church at Jerusalem, and all except the apostles were scattered throughout Judea and Samaria (Acts 8:1).

We know about Stephen and how Saul witnessed his death. But have you ever caught what happened next? Great persecution broke out against the church and they all were scattered except the apostles. God got them out of there and into the world where they needed to be in the first place, and He had to use persecution to do it.

The majority of pastors these days feel like one of those jugglers who spins a plate on a stick. He gets one plate going, then puts up another. Quickly, he moves to a third. About the time he gets ready to put up plate four, he has to run back and give plates one through three a spin. Plate four gets going, maybe five, but then plates one through three have to have another spin. Starting on plate six, he notices plate four has started to wobble. Just as he gives plate four another injection of energy, plate two starts to topple. Reaching it just in time, plate six starts teetering on the edge. Finally, he is expending all his energy just keeping a limited number of plates going.

Pastors across America are doing that every day. One particular day stands out in my mind when a dear member in my congregation was dying of cancer. I was called by the family when it seemed the end was imminent. Just before I could get out the door, the phone rang. One of my spinning plates wanted to call and complain about some trivial thing in church. Someone had said something that upset their already wobbling sense of balance. I put the best spin on them I could and left. It dawned on me on the way to the hospital that this person, who knew his brother was dying, did not ask about him or even go to the hospital to check on him or his family. All that mattered was his own self-centered need. I assure you, his complaint was petty and small-minded. But, he had a "meet my need or else" mind-set. In all the years I knew him, he never won anyone to Jesus. He probably drove some away from the church.

God will not pour out His Spirit on a situation like that. Why should He? What are we going to use an outpouring for? To bless each other? Speak in tongues to each other? Heal each other until we are too old to walk around? Prophesy to each other about how good God is? Preach about how soon Jesus is coming? If that is all the out-pouring of the Holy Ghost is about, why bother? Why would God even be concerned with getting us into position for a move of His Spirit?

As I see it, Jesus gave one major reason for sending the Holy Spirit. Look closely:

> "But you will receive power when the Holy Spirit comes
> on you; and you will be my witnesses in Jerusalem, and
> in all Judea and Samaria, and to the ends of the earth"
> (Acts 1:8).

The power comes so we can be a witness to Jesus. There is nothing wrong with getting our needs met by the power of God, but the main purpose is so we can be His witness when it is over. There is nothing wrong with rejoicing and exalting the name of the Lord so powerfully we leave feeling elated and lifted up, just as long as we are witnesses to Jesus after it is all over. There is nothing at all wrong with speaking in tongues as the Spirit gives the utterance—that's the initial sign in the experience we call being baptized in the Holy Ghost. However, if that's all there is to this experience, if it all ends when we leave the altar, then something is missing. We haven't received the same thing they received on the Day of Pentecost in Acts 2.

What would happen if we all decided to put Jesus and others first? What would happen if, instead of fussing and fuming over the trivial incidents associated with a local church, we prayed for lost men and women until tears soaked the carpet? Imagine what would happen if, for one year, everyone in a local church decided to really seek God—teaching classes, singing in choirs, visiting sick and shut-in people, inviting everyone they knew to church, praying until they touched heaven, giving of their income through tithes and offerings, making a real effort to come to church and worship, touching their neighbors with love and compassion for Jesus. I will tell you what would happen— God would pour out His Spirit on that church in ways that would boggle our minds!

What Can We Do?

I would say we need to get hungry for a move of God like we hear about, but are not currently experiencing in our lives. We need to quit making excuses, lay aside all our pet reasons about why it can't happen in our lives or in our church, and just get hungry for God. There's a wonderful promise made to those who get hungry: "Blessed are those who hunger and thirst for righteousness, for they will be filled" (Matthew 5:6).

Hunger is the missing ingredient. We have great singing, wonderful teaching, powerful preaching and fantastic church facilities. We are organized, trained, polished and ready, but we just aren't hungry yet. We are not yet yearning for an outpouring of His Spirit.

What are we hungry for? We are looking for success, recognition and more comfort so we can sleep better during preaching, and our favorite songs so we can enjoy the services more. Do we hunger for our church to be bigger and better just so we can have a sense of pride about what "we have done"?

Where is our hunger for God—not for the "stuff" of God, but God. We don't have to hunger for miracles or something spectacular. That leads to carnality and earthly longings. When we yearn for God and He shows up, there will be more manifestations than we can handle!

Hunger will compel us to cast off all the things we have put in His place and find Him. The insatiable hunger for God is the only hope we have of seeing an outpouring in our land, in our church and in our personal lives.

We can start to worship—really worship—by surrendering our lives in adoration to Jesus and waiting on Him to pour out His Spirit upon us. It will work—it has to work.

When we lay our lives down for the Lord and become servants of Jesus, it might mean a change in our week or some extra time on a Sunday. It might even mean rethinking what church is all about for some of us. But it is our only hope of having an outpouring of His Spirit.

The words of Jesus apply so fittingly to our generation:

"Neither do men pour new wine into old wineskins. If they do, the skins will burst, the wine will run out and the wineskins will be ruined. No, they pour new wine into new wineskins, and both are preserved" (Matthew 9:17).

The old wineskin had become brittle and unmanageable. You could not put new wine into the container because it would not allow for the movement of fermentation on the inside. It simply could not contain what was happening within. Jesus likened us to a stale, brittle, intractable wineskin. He told us how useless we become when we get in such a condition. God is not going to pour the new wine of a fresh anointing into a container that will waste the precious contents of His anointing.

Of course, that leaves many of us in a scary predicament, wondering, *Is there any hope for us?* Yes there is hope, but only if we are willing to be made new by the hot oil of His presence. They dipped the old, brittle wineskin in hot oil and hand-rubbed it, making it pliable and useful. Only those skins that were beyond repair were discarded.

In a similar manner, God will dip us in the hot oil of His Spirit. It might be uncomfortable, but if we want to be a part of what He is doing in the last days, we will endure. We will have to patiently bear up under the strong rubbing of His presence. It will take some strength out of us. It will remove some wrinkles from our theology and philosophy and reshape what we have regarded with pride. But it is absolutely essential to undergo this process if we are to be filled with His Spirit.

I, for one, am ready to be dipped in God's holy anointing oil and made anew. Anyone ready to go with me?

12

I Will Come Again

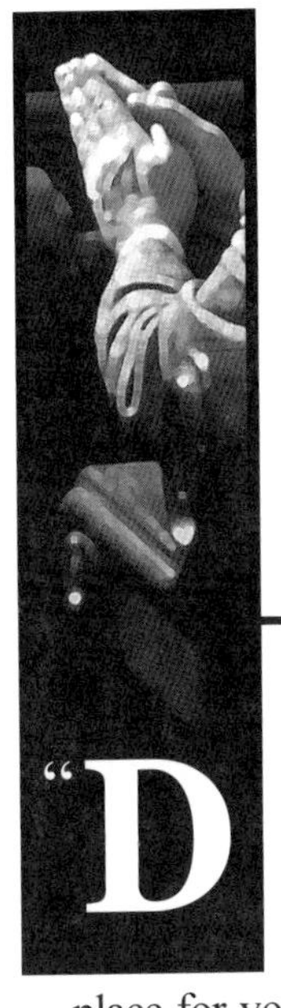

"**D**o not let your hearts be troubled. Trust in God; trust also in me. In my Father's house are many rooms; if it were not so, I would have told you. I am going there to prepare a place for you. And if I go and prepare a place for you, I will come back and take you to be with me that you also may be where I am" (John 14:1-3).

Over and over, we have pondered the question, "Can God move here?" We all know the answer is yes. The move of God in our particular situation is dependent upon many variables, such as our preparation and readiness.

God is ready when we are, but there is one more move of God (you might call it the ultimate move of the Lord) we need to prepare for. It's called the second coming of Christ. Unlike the fiery move of the Holy Spirit in revival, this movement of God has already been determined, and is even now being prepared for in the eternal decrees of the Father. Jesus made it clear that the Father knows when it is going to happen: "No one knows about that day or hour, not even the angels in heaven, nor the Son, but only the Father"(Matthew 24:36).

I don't know when He will come. The predictors and prophecy specialists don't know when He is coming. The angels that inhabit heaven don't know when this wonderful day will come. Even Jesus, when He walked on the earth, didn't know when His return would take place. But the Father knows. He has it circled on His heavenly calendar.

It will unfold something like this: At some point in history, possibly today, things will kick into high gear in the heavenlies. Angels will shout, trumpets will blast, and the spirits of saints gone on in death will fly back into resurrected bodies. Those who are alive and are prepared will suddenly change into immortal beings, equipped for a quick journey into heaven. Fast as a flash of light, we will be transported from this earthly plane into a heavenly dimension. Rather than lamenting earthly cares, we will suddenly feel the presence of millions of angels, singing in glorious harmony of the worthiness of the Lord Jesus.

It's hard to grasp just how great it will be. Think about it for a moment . . .

- Some poor saints, sick and dying, hearing only the whirring of machines and beeping of alarms over the muffled whimpers of loved ones will instantly hear shouts of joy as their sick bodies are changed into bodies like the Lord's!

- Children of God, arrested, abused, abandoned and alone, will suddenly leave the confines of their cells and join with millions of others who have been set free.

- Christians, struggling to maintain their testimony in a godless and evil world, will, in a moment's notice, be set free to live in glorious power and praise before the Lord forever.

- Widows are going to meet their husbands who died in the Lord years ago. Parents are going to meet children lost to disease and injury decades before. Children are going to be reunited with parents who had to leave them in previous days.

- Friendships that were severed much too early in life will be granted an eternity to resume.

- We will see Jesus!

Frankly, it doesn't get any better than that. This causes us to echo the sentiments of the Revelator while on the isle of Patmos, "Come, Lord Jesus!"

So why isn't the church excited over the prospects of the Lord's soon return? For many, the idea of Jesus coming back today has been tucked and neatly folded away, like a cherished Christmas ornament we plan to use again next year. Actually, the idea of Jesus coming back should be more like a daily newspaper in our lives than a Christmas ornament. It should be the paramount thought in our minds every new day of our lives.

The promise of the coming of the Lord was at the forefront of our thinking 25 years ago. We sang about it, prepared for it, longed for it—even expected it. But it didn't happen and the 80's came roaring through and made us much more comfortable. Our thinking shifted from leaving here to staying put and taking over. We stopped planning on making heaven our home and started strategizing about staying here and making earth a heaven all its own.

I know Jesus wants us to conquer. Paul told us we are more than conquerors. Jesus promised certain blessings on those who overcome in this life. But the whole time we are doing all this conquering, changing, correcting, challenging and cooperating—we need to remember one thing—Jesus is coming back and it could be today!

You don't think people are interested in end-time events? Check out the *Left Behind* series, by Jerry Jenkins and Tim LaHaye. This series has appeared consistently on the nation's best-seller lists. A quick computer check of *Amazon.com*'s best-selling list had the latest addition to the *Left Behind* series of books at number three. And it isn't even in print yet!

Perhaps it's time the church catch on one more time and prepare for what could be the next great move of God—the coming of the Lord!

It's Time for a Balanced Doctrine of Imminence

By imminence, I mean the understanding that Jesus could come back at any moment. The event described by Paul, called the Rapture by those who hold to this doctrine, could take place while you are reading this page. It is the wonderful series of events described in 1 Thessalonians 4:

> Brothers, we do not want you to be ignorant about those who fall asleep, or to grieve like the rest of men, who have no hope. We believe that Jesus died and rose again and so we believe that God will bring with Jesus those who have fallen asleep in him. According to the Lord's own word,

we tell you that we who are still alive, who are left till the coming of the Lord, will certainly not precede those who have fallen asleep. For the Lord himself will come down from heaven, with a loud command, with the voice of the archangel and with the trumpet call of God, and the dead in Christ will rise first. After that, we who are still alive and are left will be caught up together with them in the clouds to meet the Lord in the air. And so we will be with the Lord forever. Therefore encourage each other with these words (vv. 13-18).

Those who hold to a pre-Tribulation Rapture believe this could take place right now. I believe it is the viewpoint called for by the Scriptures, especially if you consider the whole theme of teaching from the Bible.

- "So you also must be ready, because the Son of Man will come at an hour when you do not expect him" (Matthew 24:44).

- "But while they were on their way to buy the oil, the bridegroom arrived. The virgins who were ready went in with him to the wedding banquet. And the door was shut. Later the others also came. 'Sir! Sir!' they said. 'Open the door for us!' But he replied, 'I tell you the truth, I don't know you.' Therefore keep watch, because you do not know the day or the hour" (25:10-13).

- "Don't grumble against each other, brothers, or you will be judged. The Judge is standing at the door!" (James 5:9).

- "Let us rejoice and be glad and give him glory! For the wedding of the Lamb has come, and his bride has made herself ready" (Revelation 19:7).

Readiness is called for—readiness to leave in a moment's notice is the proper stance. It is difficult to be ready to leave if all you are doing is fighting with someone over when the trip is going to take place. If your stance on the sequence of events doesn't exactly line up with that of a fellow believer, cut him some slack. After all, everyone can't be right about every minute detail of prophecy like you and me, can they?

Tree Climbers or Cave Dwellers?

The reason we must have a balanced doctrine of imminency is because we are so prone to go to extremes. David Jeremiah, in his book *Jesus' Final Warning,* relates the story of William Miller and his followers. It seems Miller came up with a foolproof way of deciphering the exact date of the coming of the Lord. Through calculations made on mounds of data, underpinned by a comet streaking across the sky, he came up with the date of March 21, 1843. That was the day Jesus was coming.

What did he and his followers do? "At midnight on the appointed day, his devoted followers donned their ascension robes, trekked into the mountains, and climbed towering trees to get as high as possible so they would have less distance to travel through the air when the Lord appeared to take them home."[1]

Sounds crazy, doesn't it? Of course, I know some people who had "Rapture parties" back in 1988 when it was proven with undeniable evidence that Jesus was coming that fall.

Tree climbers are all around us. They get so worked up over the dates when Jesus is going to come that they lose all sense of the normalcy of life. By their reckoning, His coming is so quickly upon us there is no time for the regular routines of life. When I was growing up, I often heard a term describing such people as being "so heavenly-minded they were no earthly good."

Paul had to deal with his own special brand of tree climbers in his day.

> We hear that some among you are idle. They are not busy; they are busybodies. Such people we command and urge in the Lord Jesus Christ to settle down and earn the bread they eat. And as for you, brothers, never tire of doing what is right (2 Thessalonians 3:11-13).

They thought since Jesus was so soon coming, they could quit working. They felt justified in just sitting around waiting on the wonderful day when Jesus would come. Paul set them straight. My translation of his admonition is, "Quit climbing trees and get to work!"

On the other hand, we have the cave dwellers. There is no way they are going to climb a tree and wait for Jesus to come. They are going to hoard up some food and guns and "hunker down 'till Jesus comes!"

During the Y2K scare, many were convinced the end was impending. One lady I pastored during that time was quite harshly upbraided by a woman in a meat market for not buying water, dried beans and some kind of Y2K meat product. When the lady from my church casually mentioned the ability of the Lord to take care of His own, she was told in no short fashion that Jesus had told her the impending crash was real and she was to get ready for it! I wonder if she has eaten all those beans and meat products yet.

Millions of us who are Spirit-filled, Bible-believing, led-by-the-Lord Christians fell prey to the paranoia that swept our land. I personally knew people who stockpiled food and water. When they asked me what was I going to do, I responded, "I'm making a list of those who have food and water. I'll just be sure to do a lot of pastoral visitation!"

Seriously, there are those who profess Jesus who have stockpiled food and are ready for tough times. My question has always been, "What are you going to do when others find out you have food? Doesn't Jesus command us to feed people when they are hungry? Doesn't shooting someone who is starving contradict the gospel?" Anyone can figure out that road leads to disaster.

God didn't call us to be cave dwellers. You can't broadcast the good news of Jesus while hiding in a cave, clutching your weapons, afraid someone might come and steal your provisions. We have been called to something higher. We have been called to be witnesses to the risen Christ to the whole earth. We are called upon to display the death and resurrection of the Lord until He comes.

I refuse to hide in a cave, fearing the Antichrist. I refuse to believe that the God who provided for an entire nation in the wilderness cannot take care of me and my needs!

Someone sent me an e-mail with the following calculations concerning the provision God had to make for Moses and the children of Israel. Just to survive, God had to send them:

- 1,500 tons of food each day. That's two freight trains a mile long, each day!

- 4,000 tons of firewood to cook the food each day. That's a few more of those mile-long trains.

- Water? 11 million gallons per day. That's a train with tanker cars some 1,800 miles long!

- In order to get them across the Red Sea in one night, God had to carve a path some 3 miles wide so they could march 5,000 abreast.

- They camped on some 750 square miles, or about two-thirds the size of the state of Rhode Island.

God did that for 40 years! We don't have to worry about tomorrow. We don't have to lose sleep wondering what will happen if Jesus doesn't come on our timetable. We don't have to sweat the tiny details of prophecy. We just have to be ready when He comes.

Being ready means going about our business and winning the world, one person at a time, for the Lord. We will never do that by going off the deep end and climbing trees or hiding in a cave. We are, however, going to make an impact on our world when we boldly proclaim the name of the Lord as the Way, the Truth and the Life.

We will touch men and women when they see us, not as escapists, but as normal men and women who have found the inner strength that enables us to stand in a godless world and maintain a readiness to leave in a moment's notice.

After all, this is our hope. As wonderful as a great revival is, it passes. The results may last for years, but the energy of the revival will pass. As great as it is to be healed, one day healing will cease and death will come to call. As glorious as blessings and prosperity are, they will one day fade from the scene when our journey here is over. Our hope is in the coming of the Lord and the glory that awaits us on the other side.

Two passages of Scripture bear this truth with power and clarity:

If only for this life we have hope in Christ, we are to be pitied more than all men (1 Corinthians 15:19).

We wait for the blessed hope—the glorious appearing of our great God and Savior, Jesus Christ (Titus 2:13).

The coming of Jesus is our hope. And He is coming! He will appear in the clouds and we will rise to meet Him. Everything else is passing. Regardless of the beauty and wonder of God's temporal blessings, they are just that, temporary. But when this blessed hope occurs, everything will change. In a moment, our lives will forever be altered by the last great move of God we will ever experience. He will come. We will go. All will be well!

If the promise of God is true, if the words of Jesus bear any weight, if the testimony of angels on the day of His ascension means anything, this hope should create in us a deep desire to live every day of our lives with this thought in every decision we make: Jesus could be coming back right now!

One thing this kind of thinking produces is confrontation. That's an ugly word to many, but it is something most of us really need. No, not a shouting confrontation, not some ugly scene on the roadside with another angry motorist, but what we need is a confrontation of our lifestyle. Is it what the Lord calls for? In other words, we need to remember Jesus is coming and only those who are prepared are going with Him.

That is borne out in the parable of the virgins, given by the Lord:

> "At that time the kingdom of heaven will be like ten virgins who took their lamps and went out to meet the bridegroom. Five of them were foolish and five were wise. The foolish ones took their lamps but did not take any oil with them. The wise, however, took oil in jars along with their lamps. The bridegroom was a long time in coming, and they all became drowsy and fell asleep. At midnight the cry rang out: 'Here's the bridegroom! Come out to meet him!' Then all the virgins woke up and trimmed their lamps. The foolish ones said to the wise, 'Give us some of your oil; our lamps are going out.' 'No,' they replied, 'there may not be enough for both us and you. Instead, go to those who sell oil and buy some for yourselves.' But while they were on their way to buy the oil, the bridegroom arrived. The virgins who were ready went in with him to the wedding banquet. And the door was shut. Later the others also came. 'Sir! Sir!' they said. 'Open the door

for us!' But he replied, 'I tell you the truth, I don't know you.' Therefore keep watch, because you do not know the day or the hour" (Matthew 25:1-13).

The Lord is trying to get a message across to us. We need to be ready at all times. Being in church is not the issue. Giving regularly is not the issue. Singing in a choir is not the issue. What's being questioned here is our personal relationship with Christ. Is it growing? Are we making provision for the journey? Are we doing our part through prayer and dedication? At the moment of His coming, that will be the only thing that matters.

We have been told plainly of our need to be ready. See if the words of John confront any areas of our lives. "Everyone who has this hope in him purifies himself, just as he is pure" (1 John 3:3).

John was speaking of the hope that accompanies the coming of the Lord. He was telling us our lives betray our hopes. If we are really ready, thinking Jesus might come back at any moment, we will be taking strides to live holy and pure lives. Today, we must all be confronted with this question: If Jesus were to come right now, am I ready? If the answer is "no," or "I'm not sure," there is no better time than right now to address this need.

Something else this eager expectation should produce in us is a challenge. If Jesus is going to come back next week, we had better get busy. Most of us will argue that we are already too busy. We scarcely have a moment left at the end of the day. Isn't it time we discover what the Lord expects of us and get busy doing His will? Here are the marching orders left by the same Jesus who is coming back again:

So when they met together, they asked him, "Lord, are you at this time going to restore the kingdom to Israel?" He said to them: "It is not for you to know the times or dates the Father has set by his own authority. But you will receive power when the Holy Spirit comes on you; and you will be my witnesses in Jerusalem, and in all Judea and Samaria, and to the ends of the earth" (Acts 1:6-8).

These are the last recorded words of the Lord before He ascended into heaven. They carry great weight for us because these words comprise His last command given to His church. I find it interesting that they were spellbound by the very same thing as we: When is Jesus coming back and all this going to end? The reply of Jesus was then, and is today, a repudiation of the clamoring and obsessive attitude captivating so many when it comes to prophecy. Jesus said, "All that, or the timing at least, is none of your business. You just get busy, and stay busy, bringing people to Me until I return."

That, my friend, is the challenge that should drive us forward. If Jesus comes today, it's fine for those of us who are ready. But what about all the others who are not? What about the coworker who doesn't yet know the joy of salvation? What about that son or daughter who has strayed from the Lord and no longer lives for God? What about the millions who still haven't heard about Jesus? Our challenge is to carry the love of God to them so they too can be ready when the Lord comes.

Finally, this promise should provide some comfort. Paul, in the promise about the rapture of the church in 1 Thessalonians, ended the description of that day with these consoling words:

"Therefore encourage each other with these words" (4:18).

The King James Version stated we should "comfort" one another with this promise. He was writing to people who were grieving. Their loved ones had died and they thought that changed the promise of God. They were looking for Jesus to come back in a few days, perhaps a few weeks, and certainly no more than a few years. When Jesus didn't fulfill their expectations, naturally, some of them grew sick and died. That upset them terribly. Where had they missed it? Was it all a joke?

Paul gave them a revelation from the Lord about how things would come to completion. He let them know that in the end, Jesus is coming back. The dead will live again. Those alive will be changed and will forever be with the Lord. That is supposed to comfort us. And it does. I have been with many families during funerals. Without exception, when the person knew Christ, the greatest comfort I could offer was this promise: Jesus is coming and you will see them again. I am glad to tell you this final move of God, the great wrapping-up of God's dealing with the church, is on schedule and will come off without a hitch. I can think of no greater source of joy and strength than to know that one day, perhaps today, the trumpet will sound and we will suddenly change residence. Before blinking an eye, we will be with Jesus forever.

Does this hope make a difference? It should change everything about your life. Max Lucado, in his book *When Christ Comes,* tells the story of Arman, a young boy who was trapped inside a collapsed school building during a terrifying and deadly earthquake in Armenia in 1989. After the shaking stopped, Arman's father ran to the shattered building. It had been leveled. Looking at the mass of stones and rubble, he remembered a promise he had made to his little son, "No matter what happens, I'll always be there for you." Driven by his promise, he found the area closest to his son's room and started rolling back rocks and debris. As other parents arrived and saw the horrible specter, they told him to stop digging. They told him to face reality—his son, along with their children, was dead. Even a policeman tried to get him to stop digging.

He refused. He dug for 36 hours. He refused to quit. Hands bleeding, energy sapped, almost exhausted to the point of collapse, he dug on for 38 hours. Finally, rolling a large stone out of the way, he heard his son's voice. When he called out Arman's name, his son answered back, "Dad, it's me, it's me!" Then the little boy added these words to his cry: "I told the other kids not to worry. I told them if you were alive, you'd save me, and when you saved me, you'd save them too."[2]

You and I can make a difference in our culture because we have the unchanging, unshakable, unvarying promise of our Lord. We know that He will come again!

As we strive to find the place where God can move freely in our lives, in our churches, let us always be prepared for the great, final move of God. Let's keep our eyes glancing heavenward. Let's keep looking for the soon return of our Lord.

Maranatha!

Endnotes

SECTION ONE

Chapter 1
[1] Leonard I. Sweet, *soulTsunami* (Grand Rapids: Zondervan, 1999) 50.

[2] Sweet, 60-61.

[3] Sweet, 62.

[4] Religion Today, *www.religiontoday.com*, 4/26/00.

[5] Lou Engle, *Digging the Wells of Revival* (Shippensburg, PA: Destiny Image, 1998) 38.

Chapter 2
[1] Taken from *Barna.org* Web site.

[2] Andy Butcher, *charismanews.com, 5/27/00.*

[3] Leonard Sweet, 42.

[4] Frank Damazio, *Crossing Rivers, Taking Cities* (Ventura, CA: Regal, 1999) 100.

Chapter 3
[1] Hugh Williams, *Fire in the Wax Museum* (Shippensburg, PA: Destiny Image, 1992) 37.

Chapter 4
[1] Benny Hinn, *Welcome, Holy Spirit* (Nashville: Thomas Nelson, 1997) 234-235.

Chapter 5
[1] Vance Havner, *Leadership*, vol. 4, no. 1; taken from *PreachingToday.com*

[2] Jon H. Allen, *New Illustration Digest*, June/July 2000.

SECTION TWO

Chapter 7

[1] R.T. Kendall, When God Shows Up: Expecting the Unexpected (Ventura, CA: Gospel Light, 1998) 120f.

Chapter 8

[1] C.S. Lewis, *the Screwtape Letters* (London: Goffrey Bles, 1942) 9.

[2] R. Kent Hughes, *Preaching the Word: Mark, vol. (Westchester, IL: Crossway, 1989) 118.*

[3] Taken from *crimelibrary.com* Web site.

[4] Taken from *crimelibrary.com* Web site.

[5] Dutch Sheets, *Intercessory Prayer* (Ventura, CA: Regal, 1997) 42.

[6] Sheets, 44.

[7] Taken from, "My Story," by David Berkowitz, *inetworld .net/testimony* Web site.

SECTION THREE

Chapter 10

[1] "Chinese Pastors Pay Big Price for Growth," *Current Thoughts and Trends*, Sept 2000: 26.

[2] *Current Thoughts and Trends*, 26.

[3] *Current Thoughts and Trends*, 26.

[4] *Current Thoughts and Trends*, 26.

[5] Jack Deere, *Surprised by the Power of the Spirit* (Grand Rapids: Zondervan, 1993) 30.

[6] Hugh Williams, *Fire in the Wax Museum* (Shippensburg, PA: Destiny Image, 1992) 126.

Chapter 11

[1] Elmer Towns and Neil T. Anderson, *Rivers of Revival* (Ventura, CA: Regal, 1997) 15.

[2] Erwin W. Lutzer, *Ten Lies About God* (Nashville: Word, 2000) xi.

[3] Richard E. Bieber, *Set Our Hearts on Fire: How to Kindle Revival in Your Church* (Ann Arbor, MI: Servant, 1998) 129-130.

[4] Ron McIntosh, *The Quest for Revival* (Tulsa: Harrison, 1997) 176.

[5] Ron McIntosh, 176.

Chapter 12

[1] David Jeremiah, *Jesus' Final Warning* (Nashville: Word, 1999) 1.

[2] Max Lucado, *When Christ Comes* (Nashville: Word, 1999) 21.